Alice & Daisy

Alice & Daisy

SPECIAL OCCASION OUTFITS
AND FURNITURE

Valerie Janitch

Photography by
Gary Sinfield

Nexus Special Interests

Nexus Special Interests Ltd.
Nexus House
Azalea Drive
Swanley
Kent BR8 8HU

First published by Nexus Special Interests Ltd., 1998

ISBN 1-85486-183-2

Designed and typeset by Kate Williams, Abergavenny.
Printed and bound in Great Britain by Biddles Ltd., Guildford & King's Lynn.

Contents

Acknowledgements   vii

Introduction, guidelines and helpful hints   1

1   *Alice and Daisy at the seaside*   5

2   *Alice's best coat and hat*   13

3   *Daisy's 'Gigi' outfit*   19

4   *Daisy is a bridesmaid*   25

5   *Alice goes shopping*   29

6   *Daisy's river picnic and Alice's garden party*   33

7   *An evening out and Alice's first ballgown*   41

8   *Alice and Daisy's accessories*   51

9   *Pretty trims for the finishing touch*   65

10   *Bertie*   69

11   *Making the furniture*   73

Stockists and suppliers   87

Acknowledgements

I would like to thank the following:

Beverly Laughlin for so enthusiastically getting this book off the ground, and **Lyn Corson** for carrying it through and being a dream editor.

Gary Sinfield, who took the charming photographs – and waited so patiently while Alice and Daisy decided what to wear!

Kate Williams for using all her imagination and skill to create such an attractive book out of a lot of practical text and drawings.

Chris Kingdom and **Rosemary Pinkney** of *Offray*, for all the lovely ribbons used to give the finishing touches to Alice and Daisy's clothes and furniture.

UHU for generously supplying all the adhesives used in this book.

Kevin McArthy of *The Cutting Edge*, for all his help.

Introduction, guidelines and helpful hints

Introduction

Alice and Daisy, the fashion-conscious rag dolls that we first met in *Alice & Daisy: Edwardian rag doll sisters to make and dress* (published by Nexus Special Interests), are growing up fast, and they're finding their basic wardrobe is inadequate for their busy life – in fact, they never seem to have a thing to wear! So here they are again, dressing up for a range of social events from a boating picnic and a garden party to a theatre visit and a grand ball. Alice also needs a smart town suit and Daisy's going to be a bridesmaid.

In case your rag dolls want a little dog like Bertie, there are the instructions for making him plus all his coats, collars, leads and top-knots. If you have been admiring the sisters' furniture you can make that too. No saws, hammers or nails are needed – just fabric-covered cardboard (often old cartons) and glue.

Guidelines and helpful hints

Here are some useful tips that will not only help to make the job easy and enjoyable, but will also ensure really professional results.

The fabrics to use

The dolls' clothes are made from small amounts of lawn, lightweight dress fabric or felt. Cotton-type fabrics are best for most things: look for a firm, close weave. Silky man-made fabrics usually fray, but if you can't avoid using them, treat the cut edges

1

with *UHU Action +* fabric glue or other fray-check product, available from haberdashery departments.

Summer dress fabrics are generally the ideal weight, and sometimes a slightly heavier cotton sheeting can be useful, but don't use thicker fabrics as they are too bulky – felt is a good alternative.

Making your patterns

Trace the patterns onto household greaseproof paper. Trace all the markings, notches and arrows, also the name of the garment and which part it is, and if it has to be reversed to cut a second piece. When only the word FOLD is shown, it indicates a fold in the fabric, but sometimes you are asked to fold the paper: in this case, trace everything through to the other side before opening it out.

You will find that large, simple shapes are shown as diagrams with measurements. Draw out the pattern using a large sheet of graph paper (or special pattern drawing squared paper from haberdashery departments). Fix the tracing paper on top, then follow the lines of the squared paper with a ruler to draw out your pattern to the specified measurements.

Following the directions

It is worth reading through the *whole* of each step, even though it may contain several operations. This will explain what you are aiming to achieve, making the method easier to understand.

Cutting out

Pin the patterns to the wrong side of the fabric, noting when a fold is necessary. The arrows indicate the straight vertical thread in woven fabrics, and should be parallel to the selvedges. Felt is not woven, so patterns can be placed in any direction.

When a pattern is marked REVERSE, turn it over to cut the second piece. If you are able to cut the pattern in double fabric (right sides together), the shape will be automatically reversed for the piece underneath.

Cut out carefully, using small pointed scissors for detailed pieces. Transfer the notches and dots to each piece of fabric, using a chalk pencil or disappearing marker.

Seams

Approximately 5 mm (¼ in) is allowed for seams on fabric, and approximately 2 mm (¹⁄₁₆ in) for felt, which should be oversewn to join (see below).

Always work with right sides together, unless otherwise stated. Pin the pieces together before stitching a seam, matching any markings. Use 2.5 cm (1 in) dressmakers' pins or, if working on a particularly delicate fabric, 'lace' or 'wedding dress' pins are finer and won't leave a mark.

Sewing

You can sew either by hand or machine, although short seams, setting-in sleeves, etc. are often quicker and neater done by hand. Felt seams should be oversewn with small stitches close together, and this is less bulky when done by hand.

Use regular sewing thread, but have it double for long lines of skirt gathers. Clip curves and corners neatly before turning: this is really vital on such small garments. Press seams open. When seams are too tiny for an iron, use your thumbnail.

Making neat hems

On lightweight fabrics, it's often possible to turn under a double hem without it looking bulky, but when working with medium-weight fabrics it is more attractive to turn hems under only once, and herringbone-stitch over the raw edge (see diagram). When doing this try, when possible, to cut the fabric straight along a thread as this will look neater and prevent fraying.

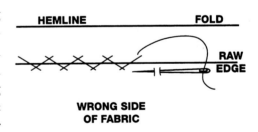

Elastic

Narrow round elastic (not shirring elastic) is best. When using it to draw up wrists, etc, herringbone-stitch over the top of the elastic with double thread, then draw it up as required and either knot or stitch the cut ends. This is neater than threading it through a channel.

Snap fasteners

The most suitable ones to use on this scale are 7 mm (¼ in) and transparent: these are thin enough to avoid bulkiness and are almost invisible. They are also flexible, which makes them easy to sew on and manipulate.

Trimmings to choose

Trimmings are the icing on the cake: lace, broderie anglaise and ribbons, with lots of braid and flowers (both of which you can make yourself). However, do keep the decoration in proportion, as you can so easily ruin the effect by using something that is too large or heavy for that garment. On the other hand, avoid very delicate lace: look for crisper lace edgings which will hold their shape. Buy the daintiest broderie anglaise (eyelet embroidery) you can find, and choose ribbons in colours that complement the garment. All the ribbons used in this book are by *Offray*, who have a wonderful range of shades, especially in single-face satin.

Glue

Trimmings are usually most easily fixed with glue. Use an all-purpose clear adhesive like *UHU*, which is quick-drying and gives a very firm hold. When you need to stick fabric to cardboard, a glue stick (like *UHU Stic*) is ideal.

Incidentally, if you hate using glue (lots of people do!), you can always stitch braid into position: nevertheless, it's a good idea to smear a little glue underneath the area before you cut across the braid (not when you cut it lengthways) to prevent it unravelling.

Chapter 1

Alice and Daisy
at the seaside

Alice's seaside dress

Just right for summer holidays and a stroll along the promenade – and so fashionable too, with its low waistline and shorter skirt – making it a good basic design for more formal occasions.

You will need:

- ✂ 30 cm (⅜ yd) medium-weight cotton-type fabric 90 cm (36 in) wide
- ✂ 12 cm (5 in) deep x 6 cm (2½ in) narrow horizontal striped fabric for the bodice insertion
- ✂ 3.5 m (4 yd) black satin ribbon, 1.5 cm (¹⁄₁₆ in) wide, for the braid
- ✂ 20 cm (¼ yd) black satin ribbon, 9 mm (⅜ in) wide, for the bow
- ✂ 90 cm (1 yd) lace, 1 cm (⅜ in) deep
- ✂ 12 cm (5 in) bias binding for the neck
- ✂ 3 snap fasteners and matching sewing threads
- ✂ UHU Action + fabric adhesive or alternative fray-check, and clear adhesive

1 Cut the front once, the back and sleeve twice each, and the skirt as Fig 1.

2 Place the bodice insertion pattern on the (horizontally) striped fabric and draw round it. Remove the pattern and go over the line with *Action +*. When dry, cut out and stitch to the dress front, as the broken line.

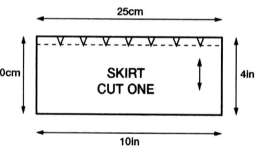

FIG. 1.

3 Join the front to the back pieces at each shoulder and press the seams open.

4 Gather each sleeve as indicated. With the right sides together, pin them into the armholes, matching side edges, notches, and centre top to the shoulder seam. Draw up the gathers to fit and stitch. Clip curves.

5 Join the side and sleeve seams.

6 Mark the top edge of the skirt equally into sixteen, then gather, beginning and ending 1 cm (⅜ in) from the side edges.

7 With the right sides together and raw edges level, pin the bodice to the skirt, matching notches and seams to the marked points. Draw up to fit and stitch. Tack the seam up under the bodice, then stitch lace on top.

8 Join the centre back seam, leaving 10 cm (4 in) open at the top. Turn under and herringbone-stitch the edges.

9   Bind the neck edge, then stitch snap fasteners at neck, centre and waist.

10 Turn under 2 cm (¾ in) hems on the sleeves and skirt, and herringbone-stitch the edges.

11 Stitch lace over the sleeve hems and over the edge of the bodice insertion, beginning and ending at the centre back (gather round the front point). Glue plaited ribbon braid (Trims: Chapter 9) round the neck, sleeves and skirt as illustrated.

12 Make a butterfly bow (Trims: Chapter 9 – points A and B each 4.5 cm [1¾ in] from the centre). Stitch over point of insertion.

Alice's seaside pantalettes

You will need:

- ✄ 20 cm × 40 cm (7½ in × 15 in) lightweight cotton-type fabric
- ✄ 40 cm (15 in) broderie anglaise, 2.5 cm (1 in) deep
- ✄ 20 cm (¼ yd) narrow round elastic and matching sewing thread

1 Cut the pantalettes pattern twice.

2 Join each inner leg seam between A–B. Turn both pieces to the right side and then, right sides together, join the two between C–A–C (Fig 2). Clip the curve.

3 Fold the top edge over, turning the raw edge under, and hem. Thread elastic through, draw up to fit and knot securely.

4 Turn up and herringbone-stitch the leg hems. Edge with broderie anglaise.

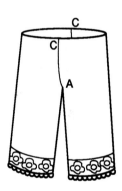

FIG. 2.

Daisy's daring bathing costume

Daisy's bathing outfit is the height of fashion, with its just-below-the-knee pantalettes and saucy satin bows! She chose a bright yellow check, but a bold stripe would have caught her holiday mood just as well.

You will need:

- ✄ 40 cm (½ yd) medium-weight cotton-type fabric, 90 cm (36 in) wide
- ✄ 70 cm (¾ yd) satin ribbon, 1.5 cm (⅝ in) wide, for the sash and hat trim
- ✄ 30 cm (12 in) satin ribbon, 1 cm (⅜ in) wide, for the pantalettes trim
- ✄ 10 cm (4 in) satin ribbon, 6 mm (¼ in) wide for the neck trim
- ✄ 12 cm (5 in) bias binding for the neck, 1 m (1 yd) narrow round elastic, matching sewing threads

1 Plan all your pattern pieces out first, to ensure your cutting plan allows sufficient fabric. Cut Alice's seaside pantalettes pattern twice (see page 11: note cutting line for the bathing costume). Cut the bodice front once and the bodice back and sleeve twice each. Cut the skirt as Fig 3, and the cap as Figs 4 and 5.

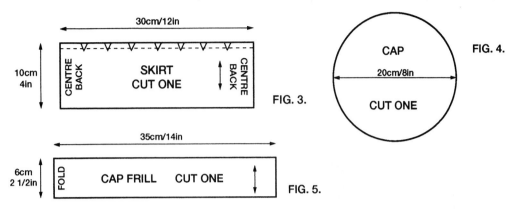

2 Follow Steps 1, 2 and 3 for Alice's pantalettes (see page 7).

3 Turn up the leg hems 2.5 cm (1 in): turn the raw edge under and hem. Then stitch again 1 cm (⅜ in) below and thread elastic through: draw up to fit and knot securely.

4 Make butterfly bows (Trims: Chapter 9) from 15 cm (6 in) lengths of ribbon, and stitch at the side of each leg.

5 Join the front to the back pieces at each shoulder. Press the seams open.

6 Gather each sleeve as indicated. With the right sides together, pin into the armholes, matching the side edges, notches, and centre top to the shoulder seam. Draw up the gathers to fit and stitch. Clip curves.

7 Join the side and sleeve seams.

8 Turn up a 1.5 cm (⅝ in) hem around the sleeves: turn under 5 mm (¼ in) and hem. Thread elastic through, draw up to fit and knot securely.

9 Mark the top edge of the skirt equally into eight. Then gather, beginning and ending 1 cm (⅜ in) from the side edges. With the right sides together and raw edges level, pin the bodice to the skirt, matching notches and seams to the marked points. Draw up to fit and stitch.

10 Herringbone-stitch a 1 cm (⅜ in) hem round the lower edge, then turn under and herringbone-stitch the edges of the back opening.

11 Bind the neck edge and trim with a butterfly bow. Stitch snap fasteners to the back opening at neck, centre and waist.

12 With the right sides together, stitch one edge of the frill around the edge of the cap: stitch join and trim off surplus. Fold frill in half lengthways, wrong side inside, turn the raw edge under and hem.

13 Place elastic on wrong side of cap, against inner edge of frill, and herringbone over it with double thread (Fig 6). Draw up to fit and knot securely.

14 Make a butterfly bow from 22 cm (9 in) ribbon and stitch at front of cap. Tie remaining ribbon round the waist.

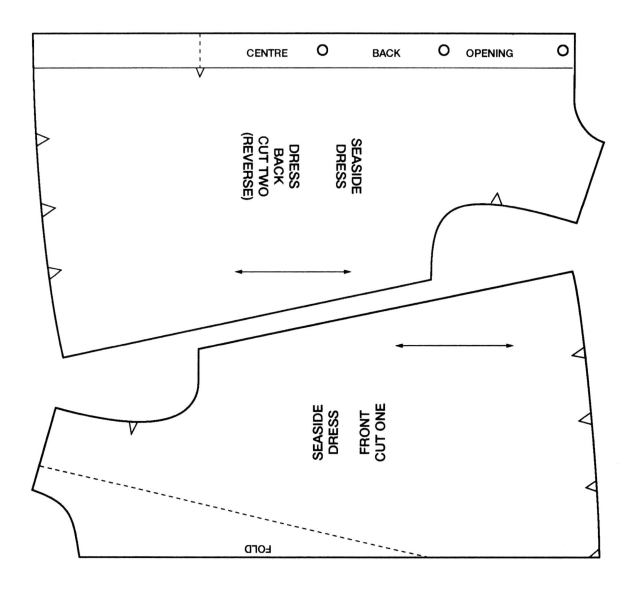

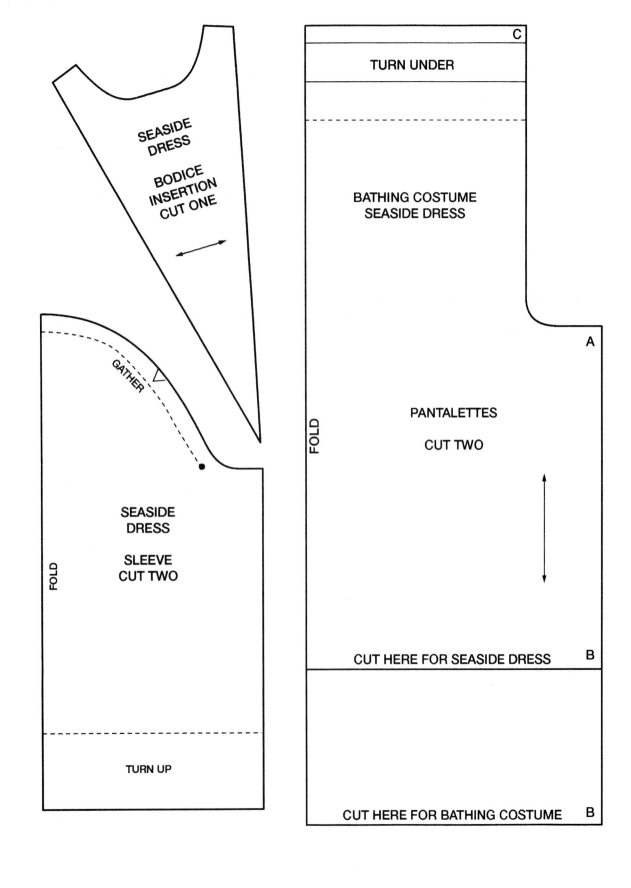

SEASIDE
DRESS

BODICE
INSERTION
CUT ONE

GATHER

SEASIDE
DRESS

SLEEVE
CUT TWO

FOLD

TURN UP

C

TURN UNDER

BATHING COSTUME
SEASIDE DRESS

FOLD

A

PANTALETTES

CUT TWO

CUT HERE FOR SEASIDE DRESS   B

CUT HERE FOR BATHING COSTUME   B

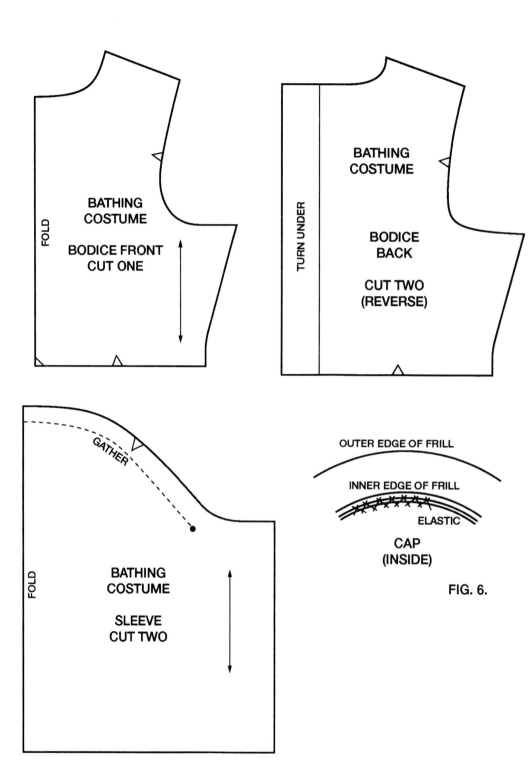

BATHING
COSTUME

BODICE FRONT
CUT ONE

FOLD

BATHING
COSTUME

BODICE
BACK

CUT TWO
(REVERSE)

TURN UNDER

GATHER

BATHING
COSTUME

SLEEVE
CUT TWO

FOLD

OUTER EDGE OF FRILL

INNER EDGE OF FRILL

ELASTIC

CAP
(INSIDE)

FIG. 6.

Chapter 2

Alice's best coat and hat

Alice chose this elegant coat and stunning hat for a winter wedding, but it's ideal for any special occasion when she wants to impress everyone with her fashion sense. The outfit is all in felt, so it's quick and easy because the seams are oversewn and you don't have to clip curves and corners. Just remember to choose a good quality felt.

You will need:

- ✂ 40 cm (½ yd) felt, 90 cm (36 in) wide
- ✂ 3.2 m (3½ yd) satin ribbon, 1.5 mm (1/16 in) wide, for the coat braid
- ✂ 2 m (2¼ yd) satin ribbon, 1.5 mm (1/16 in) wide, for the hat braid
- ✂ 25 cm (¼ yd) grosgrain ribbon, 5 mm (¼ in) wide, for the knotted bows
- ✂ 1.8 m (2 yd) satin ribbon, 12 mm (½ in) wide, in EACH of three shades, for the roses
- ✂ 4 snap fasteners and matching sewing threads
- ✂ Thin card for the hat
- ✂ Dry stick adhesive for the hat (optional)
- ✂ *UHU Action* + fabric adhesive or alternative fray-check (optional) and clear adhesive

1 Cut the bodice back, the skirt back and the collar once each. Cut the bodice front, the skirt front and the sleeve twice each.

2 Join the bodice back to the front pieces at the shoulders.

3 Gather each sleeve as indicated. With the right sides together, pin into the armholes, matching the side edges, notches and centre top to the shoulder seam. Draw up the gathers to fit, and stitch. Check length of sleeves and shorten if necessary.

4 Gather across the skirt back, as indicated. With the right sides together and cut edges level, pin the bodice back to the skirt, matching the notches. Draw up to fit, and stitch. Join the skirt fronts to the bodice in the same way (note gathering line).

5 Join the sleeve and side seams.

6 Herringbone-stitch a 1.5 cm (⅝ in) hem around the skirt. Turn the front edges under, and herringbone-stitch.

7 With the right sides together, oversew one long edge of the collar round the neck, overlapping 3 mm (⅛ in) at each end. Fold the collar in half lengthways, right side inside, and oversew the ends. Turn to the right side and slip-stitch the second long edge over the previous one.

8 Stitch snap fasteners at the top, centre and bottom of the bodice, and halfway down the skirt.

9   Glue two lengths of plaited braid (Trims: Chapter 9) side-by-side down the right front of the coat, and single braid all round the collar.

10   Cut the grosgrain ribbon equally into three. Make a tight knot in the centre of each piece and trim the ends neatly (seal if necessary): stitch one on top of each bodice snap fastener.

11   Cut the hat crown in felt as Fig 1 and gather all round, close to the edge. Glue an 11 cm (4¼ in) diameter circle of card in the centre.

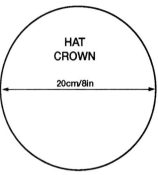

FIG. 1.

12   Cut the brim in card as Fig 2. Glue to felt with stick adhesive, then cut the felt 3 mm (⅛ in) away from both the inner and outer edges of the card. Repeat to cover the other side. Oversew the overlapping felt all round the outer edge.

13   Mark the inner edge of the brim and outer edge of the crown equally into sixteen. With the card circle inside, pin together, matching the marked points. Draw up the gathers evenly and stitch together (Fig 3).

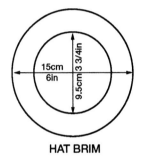

HAT BRIM

FIG. 2.

14   Make fifteen ribbon roses (Trims: Chapter 9), five in each shade, from 30–35 cm (12–14 in) lengths of ribbon. Glue all round the hat as illustrated, and glue plaited braid round the brim, over the stitches.

See Chapter 8 (Accessories) for Alice's muff and reticule.

FIG. 3.

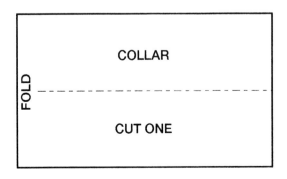

COLLAR

FOLD

CUT ONE

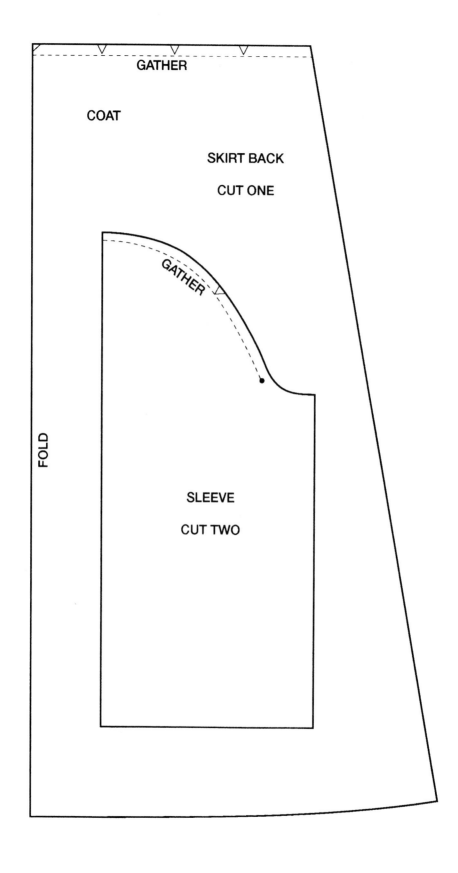

GATHER

COAT

SKIRT BACK

CUT ONE

GATHER

FOLD

SLEEVE

CUT TWO

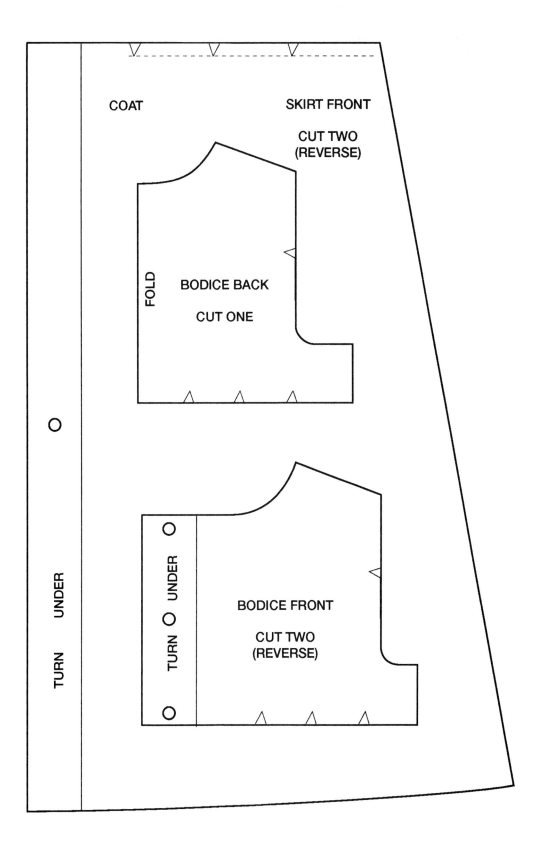

Chapter 3

Daisy's 'Gigi' outfit

Dedicated follower of fashion Daisy just had to try the latest 'Gibson Girl' look. She loved the striped shirt with its smart cravat, the plain fitted skirt, tightly belted to show off her tiny waist, and the neat little boater. Alice said she looked like a French school-girl, and laughingly called her Gigi!

You will need:

- ✄ 15 cm × 75 cm (6 in × 30 in) light/medium-weight fabric for the shirt
- ✄ 23 cm × 70 cm (9 in × 28 in) medium-weight fabric for the skirt
- ✄ 50 cm (⅝ yd) black satin feather-edge ribbon, 9 mm (⅜ in) wide, for her belt plus 90 cm (1 yd) for her hat
- ✄ 20 cm (¼ yd) narrow round elastic
- ✄ 3 snap fasteners for the shirt, and another for the skirt
- ✄ Matching sewing threads

1 Cut the shirt front, collar and cravat once each (note direction of arrows for collar and cravat). Cut the sleeve and back twice each.

2 Join the front to the back pieces at each shoulder. Press the seams open.

3 Gather each sleeve as indicated. With the right sides together, pin into the arm-holes, matching side edges, notches, and centre top to the shoulder seam. Draw up the gathers to fit and stitch. Clip curves.

4 Join the sleeve and side seams. Turn under and herringbone-stitch a narrow hem round the lower edge.

5 With the right sides together and raw edges level, pin the collar evenly round the neck, centres matching. Stitch neatly, then trim off any excess and clip the curved edge.

6 Turn under and herringbone-stitch the edges of the centre back opening, and tack the collar to correspond. Wrong side inside, fold the collar in half lengthways, turn under the raw edge and slip-stitch over the previous stitching line. Oversew the ends. Stitch snap fasteners at collar, centre and waist.

7 Join the side edges of the cravat with tiny stitches for the centre back seam: trim the raw edge and fold as Fig 1, then stitch across the bottom. Trim and clip this seam, then turn to the right side and tack the bottom. Gather all round the top edge, beginning and ending at the seam, then turn the top edge inside, folding along the gathering line, and tack. Press, then draw up and stitch to the shirt front below the collar.

FIG. 1.

8 Turn up each sleeve 1 cm (⅜ in): turn the raw edge under and hem. Thread elastic through, draw up to fit and knot securely.

9 Cut the skirt front once and the back twice.

10 Join the side seams, and the back seam, leaving it open above the notch. Gather round the top edge.

11 With the right sides together and raw edges level, pin the waistband to the skirt, matching seams and notches. Draw up to fit and stitch.

12 Turn under and herringbone-stitch the edges of the back opening: tack the waist-band to correspond. Wrong side inside, fold the waistband in half lengthways, turn under the raw edge and slip-stitch over the previous stitching line. Oversew the ends.

13 Stitch ribbon to the waistband, level with the top edge – and repeat level with the lower edge, turning the cut ends under. Stitch a final length along the centre, over-lapping the first two.

14 Fit the skirt on the doll to mark the waist and length. Stitch the fastener into place and herringbone-stitch the hem.

To make her hat, see Chapter 8 (Accessories).

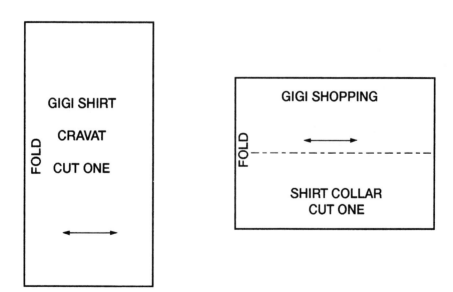

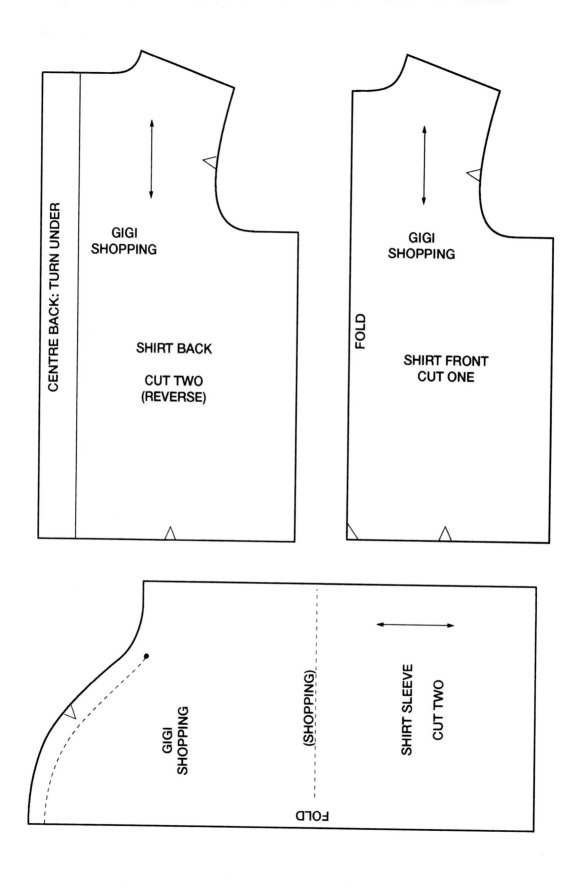

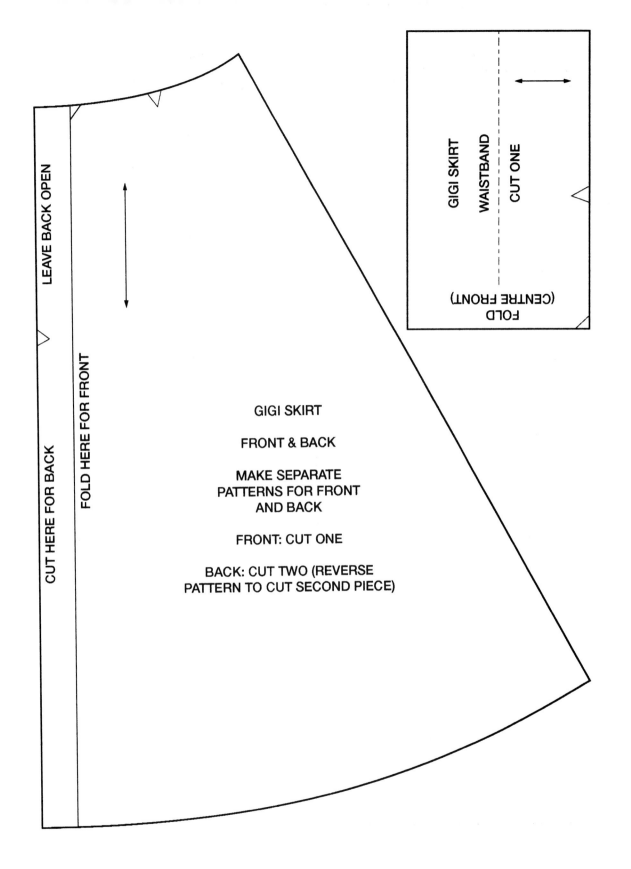

LEAVE BACK OPEN

CUT HERE FOR BACK

FOLD HERE FOR FRONT

GIGI SKIRT

FRONT & BACK

MAKE SEPARATE
PATTERNS FOR FRONT
AND BACK

FRONT: CUT ONE

BACK: CUT TWO (REVERSE
PATTERN TO CUT SECOND PIECE)

GIGI SKIRT

WAISTBAND

CUT ONE

FOLD
(CENTRE FRONT)

Alice and Daisy enjoy a sunny day beside the sea – but Bertie won't behave!

Daisy plans a quiet morning walk. Alice and Bertie are going shopping.

Daisy's off for a picnic but Alice is too exhausted after her shopping trip.

Daisy tries on her bridesmaid's dress while Bertie is still deciding what to wear.

Alice is braving the winter weather but Bertie's staying home with Daisy!

Daisy helps Alice to prepare for the garden party. Really Alice – that hat!

The sisters try to explain to Bertie that he can't go to the theatre with them.

Alice is leaving for the ball and Bertie thinks she's too beautiful for words!

Chapter 4
Daisy is a bridesmaid

Daisy was so excited about being a bridesmaid and could hardly wait to try on her frock
– when she did, she looked almost as lovely as the bride herself! Daisy's simple dress is
deep cream cotton seersucker with matching lace. A pearl circlet and posy of cream
roses complete her outfit for the big day.

You will need:

- ✄ 30 cm (12 in) medium-weight cotton-type fabric, 90 cm (36 in) wide
- ✄ 2.3 m (2¾ yd) lace, 1.5 cm (⅝ in) deep, to trim the neck, sleeves and hem
- ✄ 1.2 m (2⅛ yd) satin ribbon, 12 mm (½ in) wide, for large roses and streamers
- ✄ 2.6 m (3 yd) satin ribbon, 9 mm (⅜ in) wide, for small roses and streamers
- ✄ 20 cm (8 in) length of large pearl beads for her headdress
- ✄ 12 cm (5 in) matching bias binding for the neck
- ✄ 20 cm (8 in) narrow round elastic
- ✄ 3 snap fasteners and matching sewing threads
- ✄ 5 cm (2 in) circle of card for her bouquet
- ✄ Green paper table napkin or face tissue for her bouquet
- ✄ Dried greenery for her bouquet (optional)
- ✄ Elastic band to fit around the head
- ✄ Clear adhesive

1 Cut the skirt as Fig 1. Cut the bodice front once and the back and sleeve twice each.

2 Join the front to the back pieces at each shoulder. Press the seams open.

3 Gather each sleeve as indicated. With the right sides together, pin into the armholes, matching side edges, notches, and centre top to the shoulder seam. Draw up the gathers to fit and stitch. Clip curves.

4 Join the side and sleeve seams.

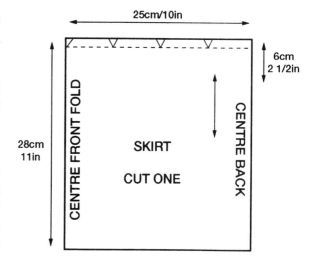

FIG. 1.

5 Turn up and tack a 1 cm (⅜ in) hem around each sleeve, then stitch lace round the edge to overlap below. Herringbone-stitch elastic over the raw edge with double thread. Draw up to fit and knot securely.

6   Mark the top edge of the skirt into eight, then gather, beginning and ending 1 cm (⅜ in) from the side edges. With the right sides together and raw edges level, pin the bodice to the skirt, matching notches and seams to the marked points. Draw up the gathers to fit and stitch.

7   Join the back seam of the skirt, leaving open 6 cm (2½ in) at the top.

8   Turn under and herringbone-stitch the edges of the back opening (bodice and skirt).

9   Bind the neck edge, then stitch lace over the binding, lower edges level, to form a stand-up collar. Gather 20 cm (8 in) lace and pin it evenly round edge-to-edge with the collar, but in the opposite direction. Draw up and stitch.

10   Sew snap fasteners to the back opening at neck, centre and waist.

11   Fit the dress on the doll to mark the length. Herringbone-stitch the hem, then stitch lace round the bottom of the skirt, with two rows above, each 5 mm (¼ in) apart.

12   Overlap and join the cut ends of the pearls to form a circle. Make a ribbon rose (Trims: Chapter 9) from 35–40 cm (14–16 in) of the wider ribbon, and two more from 25–30 cm (10–12 in) of the 9 mm (⅜ in) ribbon. Stitch the larger rose over the circlet join, with a smaller one at each side. Fold 40 cm (½ yd) of the wider ribbon in half and stitch under the large rose for streamers. Cut the ends in an inverted V-shape. Hold the circlet in place with an elastic band taken over the top of the head and underneath the hair.

13   Make a large rose and six small ones for her posy. Place the card circle in the centre of the napkin or tissue and draw the edges smoothly together underneath: bind tightly with thread to form a mushroom shape. Bind again 2 cm (¾ in) below and cut off the surplus. Glue the large rose in the centre of the covered circle, with the smaller ones round it, adding bits of dried greenery between. Tie 20 cm (¼ yd) of the narrower ribbon round the back for streamers, cutting the ends as before.

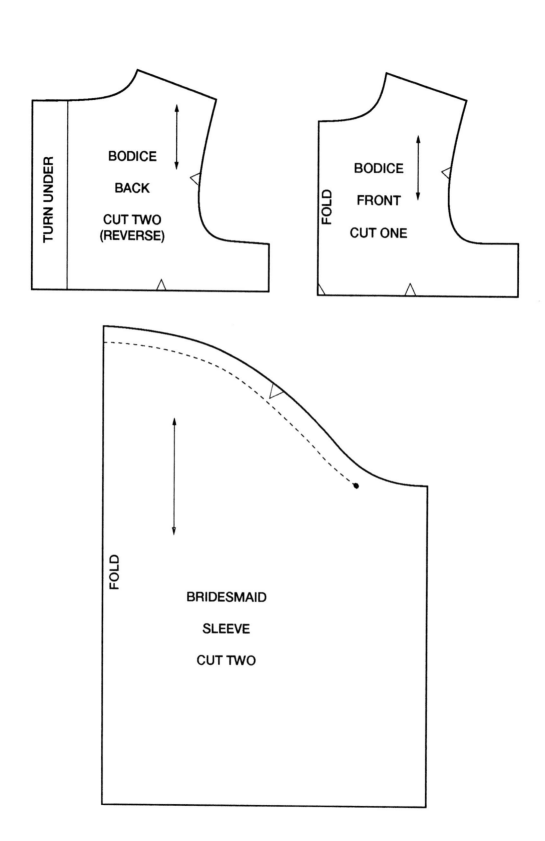

TURN UNDER

BODICE

BACK

CUT TWO
(REVERSE)

FOLD

BODICE

FRONT

CUT ONE

FOLD

BRIDESMAID

SLEEVE

CUT TWO

Chapter 5

Alice goes shopping

Alice is off to town to buy a new hat. Her tailored suit is the latest fashion: a braid-trimmed bolero jacket and matching skirt, worn over a blouse and underskirt in toning colours (see photograph on page 61). The distinctive trimming is a 1 cm (⅜ in) wide braid which can be cut down the centre to make two lengths half the width (see the photograph overleaf). If you can't find a similar braid, either buy or make a narrow one, and glue two pieces side-by-side where the full width is called for.

You will need:

- ✂ 15 cm × 75 cm (6 in × 30 in) lightweight cotton-type fabric for the blouse
- ✂ 20 cm × 40 cm (8 in × 16 in) medium-weight cotton-type fabric for the underskirt
- ✂ 20 cm (¼ yd) felt, 90 cm (36 in) wide for the bolero and overskirt, and hat OR three 20 cm (8 in) squares of felt, plus two more for the hat
- ✂ 40 cm (½ yd) lace, 5 mm (¼ in) deep, for the blouse
- ✂ 1.25 m (1⅜ yd) lace, 1.5 cm (⅝ in) deep, for the blouse and hat
- ✂ 60 cm (¾ yd) black feather-edge ribbon, 9 mm (⅜ in) wide for the skirt, hat and umbrella
- ✂ 2.4 m (2¾ yd) black braid, approximately 1 cm (⅜ in) wide, to trim the bolero and overskirt (as above) and the hat OR 4.8 m (5½ yd) black braid, approximately 5 mm (¼ in) wide (see above)
- ✂ 20 cm (¼ yd) narrow round elastic
- ✂ 4 snap fasteners, matching sewing threads and clear adhesive

1 Use the pattern for Daisy's Gigi shirt (Chapter 3) to make the blouse. Cut the front and collar once, and the back and sleeve (full length) twice each.

2 Stitch two lengths of the wider lace vertically edge-to-edge down the centre of the blouse front. Stitch a horizontal band of the narrow lace across each sleeve as the broken line on the pattern (see photograph on page 61).

3 Follow Chapter 3, Steps 2, 3, 4, 6 and 7 for the Gigi shirt (omit Step 5).

4 Turn up and tack a 5 mm (¼ in) hem around each sleeve. Turn to the right side and stitch the wider lace round the edge to overlap below. Then stitch another row above, edge-to-edge.

5 Herringbone-stitch elastic on the wrong side, over the raw edge, with double thread. Draw up to fit and knot securely.

6 Gather the remaining narrow lace and pin it evenly along the top edge of the collar to form a tiny up-standing frill: draw up and stitch.

7 Stitch snap fasteners to the back opening at collar, centre and waist.

8 Mark the top edge of the underskirt equally into eight, then gather, beginning and ending 5 mm (¼ in) from the side edges. Pin to the blouse, right sides together and raw edges level, matching the marked points to notches and seams. Draw up to fit and stitch.

9 Join the back seam of the underskirt. Fit on the doll to mark the length, then herringbone-stitch the hem.

10 In felt, cut the skirt panel five times, the jacket back and waistband once each, and the sleeve and front twice each.

11 Join the skirt panels side-by-side between the notches, oversewing the edges of the felt with tiny stitches. Press flat before joining the first and last panels, leaving 7 cm (2¾ in) open at the top.

12 Gather the top edge of the skirt. Measure your doll's waist (over the blouse) and cut the waistband this length, then mark into five equal sections. Pin over the right side of the skirt, matching the marked points to the seams, the waistband overlapping the gathers about 2 mm (¹⁄₁₆ in). Draw up to fit and slip-stitch the waistband to the skirt.

13 Cut ribbon 4 cm (1½ in) longer than the waistband and stitch on top, overlapping 1 cm (⅜ in) at one end, and 3 cm (1⅛ in) at the other. Turn the shorter overlap under the band and stitch. At the other end turn the ribbon under 1 cm (⅜ in) beyond the band, and stitch a fastener to the overlap.

14 Oversew the jacket back to the front pieces at the shoulders and press. Oversew the sleeves into the armholes between the double notches, matching the centre notch to the shoulder seam. Press, join the side seams and press again.

15 If you have the type of braid illustrated, glue a 20 cm (8 in) length over a skirt seam joining the skirt panels from under the waistband to where the panels divide: cut the remaining braid in half along the centre and glue each half down to the bottom of each panel. Repeat all round. Alternatively, use a narrow braid approximately 3–5mm (⅛–¼ in) wide (see above and Chapter 9).

16 Trim the jacket with full-width braid round the sleeve edges, then cut in half for the outer edge and all round the armholes.

To make Alice's hat, purse and umbrella, see Chapter 8 (Accessories).

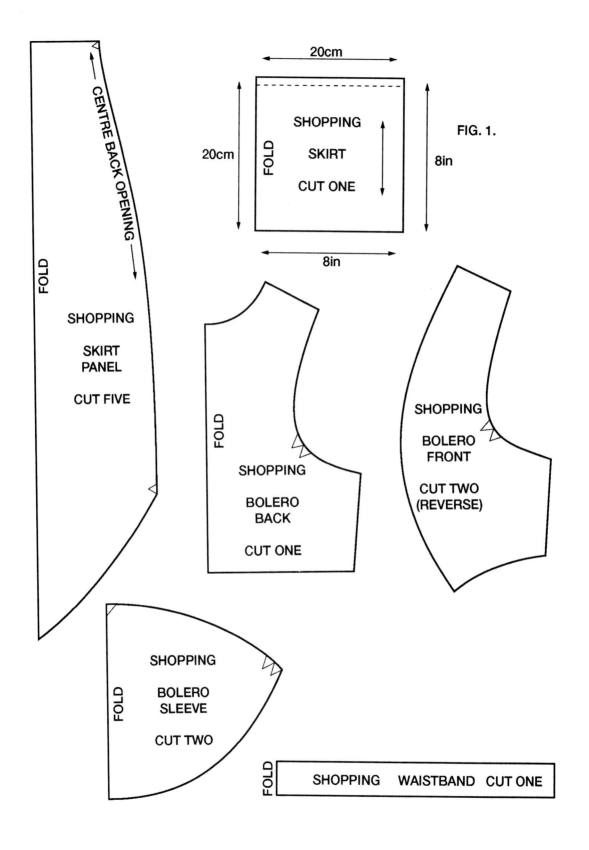

CENTRE BACK OPENING

FOLD

SHOPPING
SKIRT
PANEL
CUT FIVE

20cm

FOLD

SHOPPING
SKIRT
CUT ONE

20cm

8in

8in

FIG. 1.

FOLD

SHOPPING
BOLERO
BACK
CUT ONE

SHOPPING
BOLERO
FRONT
CUT TWO
(REVERSE)

FOLD

SHOPPING
BOLERO
SLEEVE
CUT TWO

FOLD

SHOPPING   WAISTBAND   CUT ONE

Chapter 6

Daisy's river picnic and Alice's garden party

Daisy's river picnic

When a picnic on the river was suggested, Daisy was quick to agree! This meant she needed something feminine and pretty, yet practical enough for grassy banks and climbing into boats – and a hat that wouldn't blow off in the breeze. See how she combined pieces from different patterns to make this charming frock.

You will need:

- ✄ 30 cm (12 in) light-to-medium weight fabric, 90 cm (36 in) wide
- ✄ 3.7 m (4 yd) lace, 1.5 cm (⅝ in) deep, to trim the dress, hat and parasol
- ✄ 70 cm (¾ yd) bias binding, approx 12 mm (½ in) wide, to trim the skirt
- ✄ 70 cm (¾ yd) satin ribbon, 15 mm (⅝ in) wide, for sleeves, hat and parasol
- ✄ 2.5 cm × 15 cm (1 in × 6 in) felt for her belt (to match ribbon and binding)
- ✄ 2.5 cm × 15 cm (1 in × 6 in) Vilene Bondaweb to back the belt
- ✄ 20 cm (¼ yd) narrow round elastic
- ✄ 4 snap fasteners and matching sewing threads

1 Using the patterns for Alice's garden party dress (see below), cut the bodice front and collar once, and the bodice back and sleeve twice each. Using the Gigi skirt pattern (Chapter 3), cut the front once and the back twice.

2 Follow Steps 3 to 6 for Alice's garden party dress (see below).

3 Turn to the right side and stitch lace round the bottom of each sleeve to extend below. Herringbone-stitch elastic on the wrong side, over the raw edge, using double thread. Draw up to fit and knot securely.

4 With the right sides together and raw edges level, stitch the collar evenly round the neck, centres matching. Trim off any excess and clip the curved edge.

5 Join the side seams of the skirt, then gather round the top edge. With the right sides together and raw edges level, pin to the bodice, matching notches and seams. Draw up to fit and stitch.

6 Join the back seam of the skirt, leaving 6 cm (2½ in) open at the top. Turn under and herringbone-stitch the edges of the back opening, tacking the collar to correspond. Wrong side inside, fold the collar in half lengthways, turn under the raw edge and slip-stitch over the previous stitching line. Oversew the ends.

7 Gather 80 cm (30 in) lace for the yoke and pin the gathered edge evenly round the bodice back and front following the dotted lines only. Draw up to fit and stitch.

8 Cut 25 cm (10 in) ribbon in half to make two butterfly bows (Trims: Chapter 9 – B and C each 3 cm [1¼ in] from A). Stitch to the sleeves.

9 Stitch binding round the hem as if to bind the edge but don't fold it over. Press it flat and stitch lace on top, easing it very slightly to allow for the flare.

10 Trace the belt pattern onto folded Bondaweb: turn over and trace through to the other side. Open out and iron onto felt. Cut along the traced lines, then remove the paper and iron a strip of dress fabric onto the back. Cut the fabric level and stitch on a snap fastener.

Instructions for Daisy's hat, Dorothy bag and parasol are in Chapter 8 (Accessories).

Alice's garden party

The girls' social life gets more and more exciting: while Daisy enjoys her picnic, Alice is off to a garden party in a very feminine outfit. Daisy felt the hat was quite outrageous – but kept her thoughts to herself since Alice's head was in the clouds anyway!

You will need:

- ✄ 30 cm (12 in) light-to-medium weight fabric, 115 cm (45 in) wide
- ✄ 4.4 m (5 yd) lace, 1.5 cm (⅝ in) deep, for the dress, hat and parasol
- ✄ 14 cm (5½ in) satin ribbon, 15 mm (⅝ in) wide, for the belt
- ✄ 30 cm (12 in) satin ribbon, 7 mm (¼ in) wide, to trim the sleeves and parasol
- ✄ 10 cm (4 in) satin ribbon, 3 mm (⅛ in) wide OR 15 cm (6 in) satin ribbon, 5 to 6mm (¼ in) wide, for the rose
- ✄ 20 cm (¼ yd) narrow round elastic
- ✄ 5 snap fasteners, matching sewing threads and clear adhesive (optional)

1   Cut the underskirt as Fig 1 and a semi-circle for the overskirt (Fig 2), then cut the bodice front, collar and waistband once, and the bodice back and sleeve twice each. Note: leave enough fabric to cut a 13 cm (5 in) circle for the parasol but don't cut it out yet.

2   Stitch a piece of lace horizontally across the bodice front, overlapping at each side, the lower edge level with the broken line on the pattern (ignore dotted lines). Stitch another piece above it, slightly overlapping to form a balanced pattern. Add two more pieces: the last will overlap, so stitch just inside the edge of the fabric. Catch the lace down round the armholes, then trim off the surplus all round.

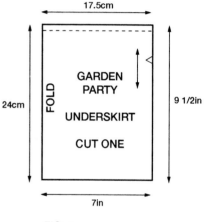

FIG. 1.

3   Join the front to the back pieces at each shoulder. Press the seams open.

4   Gather each sleeve as indicated. With the right sides together, pin into the armholes, matching side edges, notches, and centre top to the shoulder seam. Draw up the gathers to fit and stitch. Clip curves.

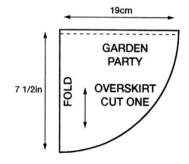

FIG. 2.

5   Join the sleeve and side seams. Try the bodice on the doll and adjust the side seams, if necessary, to give a smooth, snug fit.

36

6 Turn up and tack a 1.5 cm (⅝ in) hem round the sleeves. For each frill, overlap two 30 cm (12 in) lengths of lace and stitch together. Join the cut ends, then gather the top edge. Mark both the lace and sleeve into eight, then pin the lace 5–10 mm (¼–⅜ in) below the raw edge, matching the marked points. Draw up and stitch.

7 Herringbone-stitch elastic over the raw edge, using double thread. Draw up to fit and knot securely.

8 With the right sides together and raw edges level, stitch the collar evenly round the neck, centres matching. Trim off any excess and clip the curved edge.

9 Mark the top edge of the skirt into eight, then gather, beginning and ending 1 cm (⅜ in) from the side edges. With the right sides together and raw edges level, pin to the bodice, matching the marked points to notches and seams. Draw up to fit and stitch. Join the back seam of the skirt, leaving open 6 cm (2½ in) at the top.

10 Turn under and herringbone-stitch the edges of the back opening (bodice and skirt), and tack the collar to correspond. Wrong side inside, fold the collar in half lengthways, turn under the raw edge and slip-stitch over the previous stitching line. Oversew the ends. Stitch lace over the collar, turning 5 mm (¼ in) under at each end.

11 Fit dress on doll to mark bodice fastenings and length. Stitch snap fasteners at neck, centre and waist.

12 Herringbone-stitch the turned-up hem, then stitch lace on top, slightly overlapping the bottom. Add two more rows, overlapping as before.

13 Gather 65 cm (26 in) lace, then stitch it half overlapping the curved raw edge of the overskirt, easing the gathers round so that the lace lies flat. Mark the top edge into eight, then gather and pin to the waistband, right sides together and raw edges level, matching the marked points, and side edges, to the notches. Draw up to fit and stitch. Turn in the ends of the waistband and tack, then fold in half lengthways, wrong side inside, turn the raw edge under and slip-stitch over the gathers. Oversew the ends and stitch half a snap fastener to the right side at each end.

14 Mark the centre on the right side of the belt ribbon (arrow on Fig 3): stitch the

FIG. 3.

FIG. 4.

37

other halves of the snap fasteners 1 cm (⅜ in) each side of the centre (Fig 3). Mark the wrong side as Fig 4 and make a butterfly bow (Trims: Chapter 9) to fasten the overskirt round the waist.

15 Make butterfly bows for the sleeves from 10 cm (4 in) lengths of ribbon (points B and C each 2.5 cm/1 in from A). Make a ribbon rose (Trims: Chapter 9) and stitch at base of collar.

See Chapter 8 (Accessories) for Alice's hat, purse and parasol.

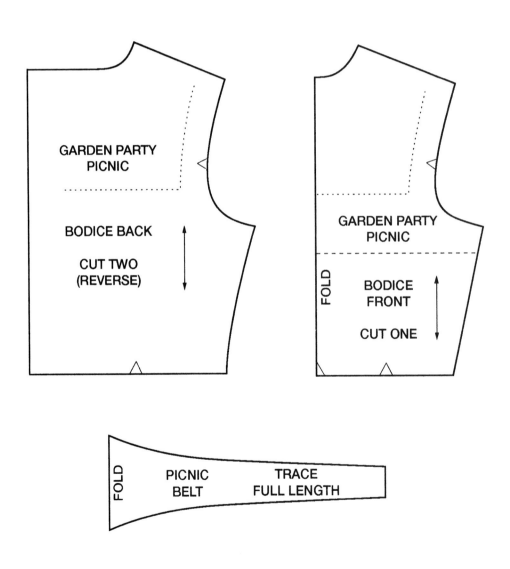

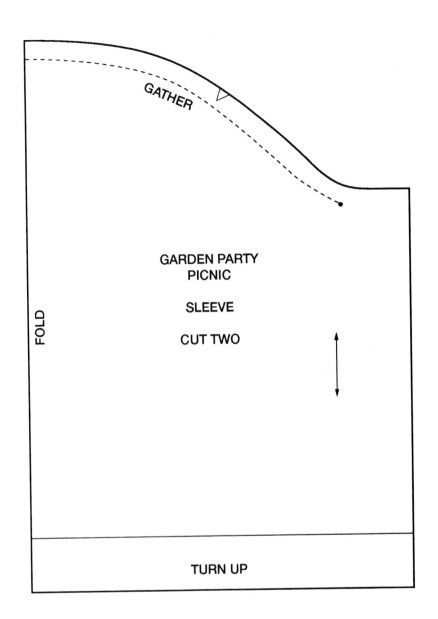

GATHER

GARDEN PARTY
PICNIC

SLEEVE

CUT TWO

FOLD

TURN UP

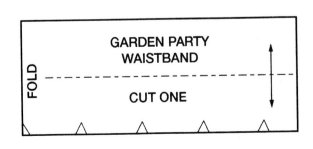

GARDEN PARTY
WAISTBAND

FOLD

CUT ONE

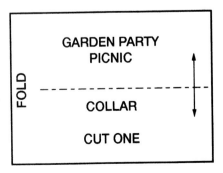

GARDEN PARTY
PICNIC

FOLD

COLLAR

CUT ONE

Chapter 7

An evening out and Alice's first ballgown

An evening out

Alice and Daisy are going to the theatre. They are determined to look extremely grown-up and elegant so the big question is – what to wear? Eventually they both decided on almost the same dress, Alice in rose and Daisy in lavender!

Alice's rose evening dress

You will need:

- ✄ 30 cm (12 in) light-to-medium weight fabric, 115 cm (45 in) or 90 cm (36 in) wide
- ✄ 1.3 m (1½ yd) lace, 2 cm (¾ in) deep, to trim her bodice, sleeves and hair
- ✄ 1.1 m (1¼ yd) embroidered ribbon, 1 cm (⅜ in) wide, for the skirt
- ✄ 10 cm (4 in) satin ribbon, 3 mm (⅛ in) wide OR 15 cm (6 in) satin ribbon, 5–6 mm (¼ in) wide, for the rose
- ✄ 2.5 cm × 15 cm (1 in × 6 in) black felt for her belt
- ✄ 2.5 cm × 20 cm (1 in × 8 in) Vilene Bondaweb to back the belt and trimming
- ✄ 20 cm (¼ yd) narrow round elastic
- ✄ A large pearl bead, and about ten small ones, for her hair
- ✄ 4 snap fasteners, matching sewing threads and clear adhesive (optional)

1 Cut the skirt and frill as Figs 1 and 2. Cut the bodice front and collar once, and the back and sleeve twice each.

2 Join the front to the back pieces at each shoulder. Press the seams open.

3 Gather each sleeve as indicated, then, right sides together, pin into the armholes, matching side edges, notches, and centre top to the shoulder seam. Draw up the gathers to fit and stitch. Clip curves.

4 Join the sleeve and side seams. Try the bodice on the doll and adjust the side seams, if necessary, to give a smooth, snug fit.

5 Turn up and tack a 1 cm (⅜ in) hem on each sleeve. Gather 30 cm (12 in) lace, and mark both the lace and sleeve into eight. Matching the marked points, pin the lace

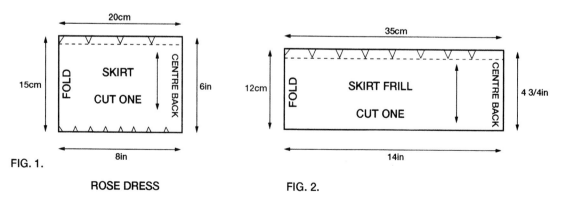

FIG. 1.

ROSE DRESS

FIG. 2.

just below the raw edge, to overlap below. Draw up the gathers and stitch. Herringbone-stitch elastic over the raw edge above the lace, using double thread. Draw up to fit and knot securely.

6   With the right sides together and raw edges level, pin the collar evenly round the neck, centres matching. Stitch neatly, trim off any excess and clip the curved edge.

7   Mark the top edge of the skirt frill and the lower edge of the skirt equally into sixteen, then gather the frill. With the right sides together and raw edges level, pin together, matching the marked points. Draw up the gathers and stitch. Turn the seam up under the skirt and tack, then stitch ribbon on top.

8   Mark the top edge of the skirt into eight, then gather, beginning and ending 1 cm (⅜ in) from the side edges. With the right sides together and raw edges level, pin to the bodice, matching the marked points to notches and seams. Draw up to fit and stitch.

9   Join the back seam of the skirt, leaving 6 cm (2½ in) open at the top. Turn under and herringbone-stitch the edges of the back opening (bodice also). Tack the collar to correspond.

10 With the wrong side inside, fold the collar in half lengthways, turn under the raw edge and slip-stitch over the previous stitching line. Oversew the ends. Stitch lace over the collar, turning 5 mm (¼ in) under at each end. Stitch snap fasteners to back opening at neck, centre and waist.

11 Gather 30 cm (12 in) lace for the yoke frill. Pin it evenly round the bodice as the broken lines, the centre front 2 cm (¾ in) below the collar, curving round so it is level with the sleeve seam over the shoulders. Draw up and stitch.

12 Follow the instructions for Daisy's belt (Chapter 6, Step 10). Trim with a scrap of bonded embroidered ribbon (about 2.5 cm/1 in long) and a rose (Trims: Chapter 9).

13 Alice put her hair up, fixing it neatly with a darning needle and matching wool, and hiding the ends with a big satin bow! A pearl-centred lace rosette added the final touch of sophistication.

Daisy's lavender evening dress

You will need:

- ✂ 30 cm (12 in) light-to-medium weight fabric, 115 cm (45 in) or 90 cm (36 in) wide
- ✂ 3.1 m (3½ yd) lace, 1 cm (⅜ in) deep
- ✂ 7.5 cm (2¾ in) matching satin ribbon, 9 mm (⅜ in) wide, for her belt
- ✂ 1.7 m (1¾ yd) single-face satin ribbon, 5–6mm (¼ in) wide, for her hair
- ✂ 8 cm (3 in) guipure or heavy lace, about 1.5 mm (⅝ in) deep, for her hair
- ✂ 2.5 cm × 15 cm (1 in × 6 in) black felt for her belt
- ✂ 2.5 cm × 15 cm (1 in × 6 in) Vilene Bondaweb to back the belt
- ✂ 20 cm (¼ yd) narrow round elastic
- ✂ 4 snap fasteners, matching sewing threads and clear adhesive

1 Cut the skirt as Fig 3. Cut the bodice front and collar once, and the back and sleeve twice each.

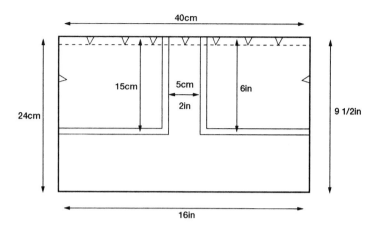

FIG. 3.

2 Follow Steps 2, 3 and 4 for Alice's rose dress.

3 Turn up and tack a 5 mm (¼ in) hem on each sleeve. Turn to the right side and stitch a row of lace round the edge of each sleeve to extend below. Stitch another row with the top edge 2.5 cm (1 in) above the first. Herring-bone-stitch elastic on the wrong side over the raw edge, using double thread. Draw it up to fit and knot securely.

4 As Alice's rose dress, Step 6.

5 Mark the bodice 5 cm (2 in) below the neck (dot on pattern). Fold 23 cm (9 in) lace in half, right side inside, and stitch as the broken line on Fig 4. Open out and press the wrong side to look like Fig 5. With the right side uppermost, position the lace with the outer point of the 'V' on the marked spot, then take the two sides up over the shoulders, the straight edge against the collar. Stitch to the bodice front and correspondingly at the back.

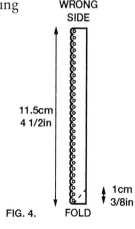

FIG. 4.

FIG. 5.

6 Stitch lace to the skirt as Fig 3.

7 As Steps 8, 9 and 10 for Alice's rose dress.

8 Fit the dress on the doll and mark the length. Herring-bone-stitch the hem, then stitch lace on the right side,

level with the lower edge. Stitch two more rows of lace between the existing ones, all the same distance apart.

9   Follow the instructions for Daisy's belt (Chapter 6, Step 10). Trim with a butterfly bow (Trims: Chapter 9).

10   Daisy piled all her hair on top (fixing it as Alice did), then tied it with a long ribbon decorated with lace and eight tiny rosebuds (Trims: Chapter 9 – use 15 cm [6 in] of ribbon for each).

Directions for the sisters' Dorothy bags are in Chapter 8 (Accessories).

Alice's first ballgown

Alice could have danced all night in her beautiful dress and everyone agreed she was the belle of the ball. She chose a pretty forget-me-not blue spotted voile trimmed with layers of frothy white lace and dainty butterfly bows, but she insisted on some black lace for a touch of sophistication. A 90 cm (36 in) wide fabric may be necessary, as there are a lot of gathers to fit into that tiny waist!

You will need:

- ✂ 45 cm (½ yd) light/medium weight fabric, 115 cm (45 in) or 90 cm (36 in) wide
- ✂ 6.4 m (7 yd) white lace, 1.5 cm (⅝ in) deep for 115 cm (45 in) wide fabric OR 5.5 m (6 yd) for 90 cm (36 in) wide fabric
- ✂ 3.4 m (3¾ yd) black lace, 1 cm (⅜ in) deep for 115 cm (45 in) wide fabric OR 2.9 m (3½ yd) for 90 cm (36 in) wide fabric
- ✂ 3.2 m (3½ yd) satin ribbon, 3 mm (⅛ in) wide for 115 cm (45 in) wide fabric OR 2.6 m (2⅞ yd) for 90 cm (36 in) wide fabric
- ✂ 20 cm (8 in) matching bias binding for the neck
- ✂ 20 cm (¼ yd) narrow round elastic
- ✂ 3 snap fasteners and matching sewing threads

1 Cut a 25 cm (10 in) deep strip across the full width of the fabric for the skirt. Cut the bodice front once and the back and sleeve twice each.

2 Join the back pieces to the front at the shoulders. Press the seams open.

3 Gather each sleeve as indicated. With the right sides together, pin into the armholes, matching side edges, notches, and centre top to the shoulder seam. Draw up the gathers to fit and stitch. Clip curves.

4 Join the sleeve and side seams. Try the bodice on the doll and adjust the side seams, if necessary, to give a smooth, snug fit.

5 Turn to the right side, then turn the top of each sleeve seam under the shoulder and top-stitch about 2–3 cm (1 in) close to the sleeve. Tidy up raw edges.

6 Turn under and tack a 3 cm (1¼ in) hem on each sleeve. Gather 35 cm (14 in) white lace and pin it evenly round, on the right side, just above the edge to extend below. Draw up to fit and stitch. Stitch flat black lace above, fractionally overlapping the white. Stitch identical rows of lace directly above.

7 Herringbone-stitch elastic on the wrong side over the raw edge, using double thread. Draw it up to fit and knot securely.

8 Mark the top edge of the skirt into sixteen, then gather, beginning and ending 1 cm (⅜ in) from the side edges (divide the gathers in half). Gather again, 5 mm (¼ in) below.

9 With the right sides together and raw edges level, pin the bodice to the skirt, matching notches and seams to the marked points. Draw up the gathers and join, stitching between the two rows.

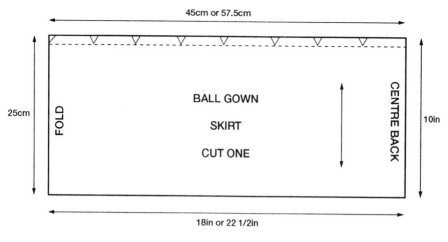

45cm or 57.5cm

25cm

FOLD

BALL GOWN

SKIRT

CUT ONE

CENTRE BACK

10in

18in or 22 1/2in

FIG. 1.

10   Join the back seam of the skirt, leaving open 6 cm (2½ in) at the top. Turn under and herringbone-stitch the sides of the back opening (bodice and skirt).

11   Make a row of tiny gathering stitches round the raw neck edge to retain the shape. Bind the edge neatly, smoothing the gathers round the back and shoulders. Then narrow the binding round the front to half-width by folding the top edge under and stitching it down inside.

12   Fit the dress on the doll to mark bodice overlap and length. Stitch snap fasteners at the top, centre and waist. Herringbone-stitch the hem.

13   Gather 2.2 m (2½ yd) white lace for a 115 cm (45 in) hem, or 1.75 m (2 yd) for a 90 cm (36 in) hem. Pin it evenly round, level with the bottom of the skirt, draw up to fit and stitch. Stitch flat black lace above as before. Repeat 2 cm (¾ in) above.

14   Gather 40 cm (16 in) white lace and pin it evenly round the neck, just below the binding. Draw up to fit and stitch. Gather 20 cm (8 in) black lace and stitch to the binding, overlapping the white.

15   Make butterfly bows (Trims: Chapter 9) from 6 cm (2⅜ in) lengths of ribbon (points B and C 2 cm [¾ in] from A). Stitch to the skirt at 5 cm (2 in) intervals, level with the top edge of the upper row of black lace. Repeat around the lower row, positioned between the upper ones. Finally, stitch one at the neck, and on each sleeve.

Directions for Alice's purse are in Chapter 8 (Accessories).

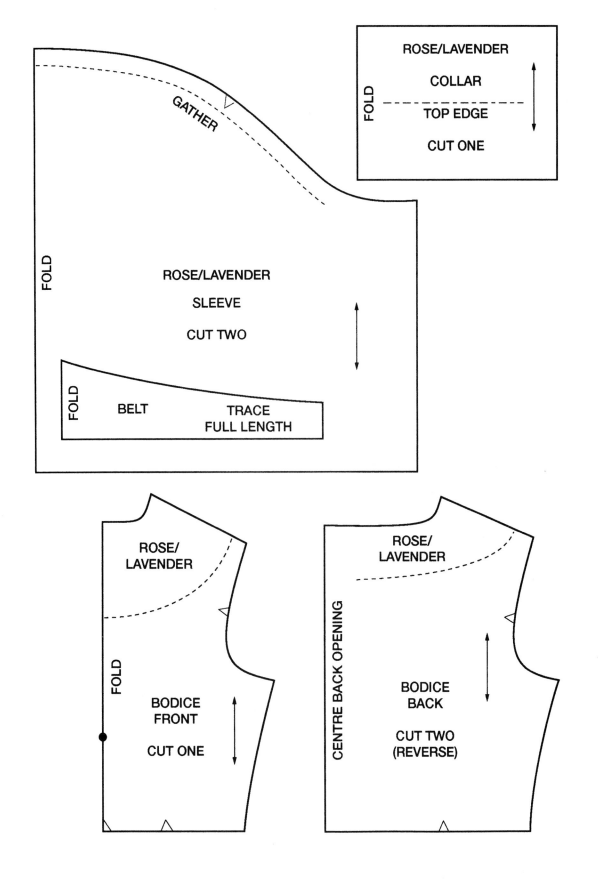

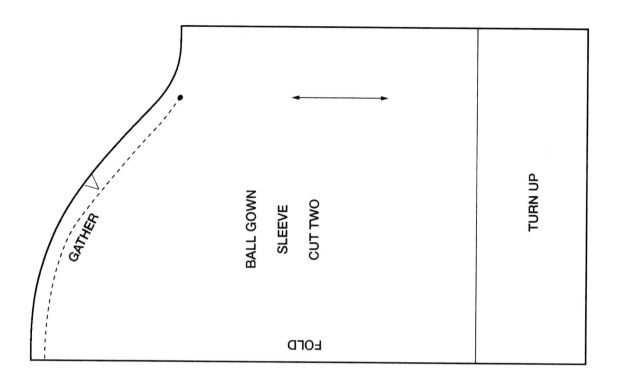

BALL GOWN

SLEEVE

CUT TWO

TURN UP

FOLD

GATHER

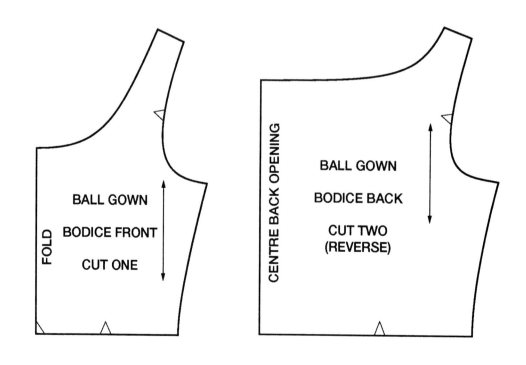

BALL GOWN

BODICE FRONT

CUT ONE

FOLD

CENTRE BACK OPENING

BALL GOWN

BODICE BACK

CUT TWO
(REVERSE)

Chapter 8
Alice and Daisy's accessories

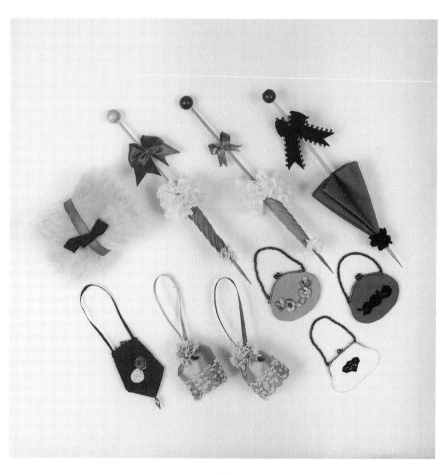

Alice's cosy fur muff (Chapter 2)

You will need:

- ✄ A 12 cm (5 in) square of fur fabric
- ✄ 12 cm (5 in) grosgrain ribbon, 5 mm (¼ in) wide, for the central band
- ✄ 5 cm (2 in) contrasting grosgrain ribbon, 5 mm (¼ in) wide, for the bow
- ✄ Matching sewing threads and clear adhesive

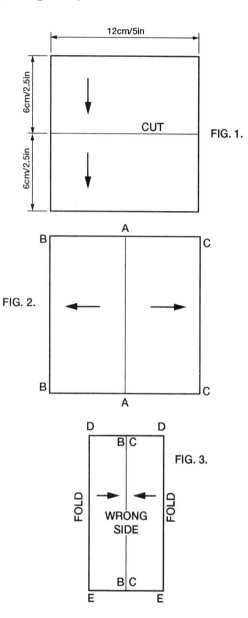

1 Cut the fur fabric in half as Fig 1 – the arrows indicate the direction of the pile.

2 Join A–A (oversew the edges), so that the pile runs as Fig 2. Then, right side inside, join B–B to C–C.

3 Turn fur side out, folding flat with the two joins level in the centre. Then, right side inside (check against arrows on Fig 3), join D–D to E–E (the two inner edges first, then the two outer ones). Turn to the right side.

4 Glue ribbon over the seam and trim with a knotted bow (see Chapter 2, Step 10).

Alice's rose-trimmed reticule (Chapter 2)

You will need:

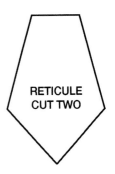

- ✂ 6 cm × 8 cm (2½ in × 3 in) felt
- ✂ 10 cm (4 in) satin ribbon, 3 mm (⅛ in) wide, for EACH rose trim
- ✂ 12–15 cm (5–6 in) satin ribbon, 1.5 mm (1/16 in) wide, for the handle
- ✂ Small round bead for the clasp
- ✂ Small oval bead, plus a tiny one, for the bottom trim (optional)
- ✂ Matching sewing threads and clear adhesive

1 Cut the reticule twice in felt.

2 With the wrong sides together, oversew neatly all round, leaving the top open.

3 Stitch the ends of the handle inside the top opening, and the clasp bead at the centre.

4 Glue two ribbon roses (Trims: Chapter 9) to one side, and anchor the oval bead to the bottom point with the tiny one.

Alice and Daisy's purses

The basic instructions are the same – only the shapes are different.

You will need:

- ✂ Scraps of medium-weight white card
- ✂ Scraps of medium-weight fabric
- ✂ 5 cm (2 in) narrow gold Russian braid
- ✂ Very tiny gilt beads for the handle
- ✂ 1 or 2 slightly larger gilt beads for the clasp
- ✂ Sewing thread to match beads
- ✂ Scrap of lace, ribbon, embroidery, etc. to trim
- ✂ Dry stick adhesive and clear adhesive

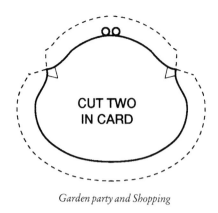

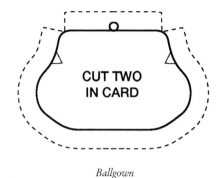

Garden party and Shopping

Ballgown

1 Cut the pattern twice in card and dry glue each to the wrong side of the fabric. Cut the fabric as the broken line, with a notch at each top corner as indicated.

2 Place both pieces right side down and spread liquid glue on the overlapping fabric. Bring it smoothly up over the edge of the card, gathering it with your fingers, and press it down on the back. Snip off uneven fabric to make the surface flatter.

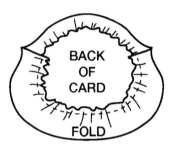

FIG. 4.

3 Cut a 2 cm × 8 cm (¾ in × 3¼ in) strip of fabric. Gather the two long edges together (don't crease the fold). Glue this strip round the lower half of one piece of card, the folded edge level with the bottom of the purse, then draw up to fit, trimming off any excess (Fig 4). Glue the other half of the purse on top.

4 Glue gold braid across the top and down to the notch, then glue clasp bead/s in the centre, and stitch a 7.5–8 cm (3 in) length of beads across the top for the handle. Glue trimming to the side.

Alice and Daisy's Dorothy bags (Chapters 6 and 7)

You will need:

- ✂ 15 cm (6 in) satin ribbon, 39 mm (1½ in) wide
- ✂ 15 cm (6 in) satin ribbon, 3 mm (⅛ in) wide, for the handle
- ✂ 25 cm (10 in) double-edge lace, 2 cm (¾ in) wide
- ✂ 2.5 cm (1 in) diameter circle of medium-weight card
- ✂ Soft toy stuffing or cotton wool
- ✂ Matching sewing threads
- ✂ Dry stick adhesive such as *UHU Stic* (optional) and clear adhesive

**FIG. 5.
DOROTHY BAG**

1   Cut off a 39 mm (1½ in) square of ribbon and dry glue the card circle in the centre, on the wrong side. Gather all round and draw up tightly to form the base.

2   With the right sides together and with tiny stitches, oversew one edge of the remaining ribbon round the base (Fig 5): trim off the excess after gluing a small overlap. Turn to the right side and stuff lightly.

3   Gather the top edge of the ribbon and draw up, stitching the ends of the handle inside.

4   Lightly glue the lace round, overlapping the lower edge a fraction. Join the remaining lace to form a circle and gather along the centre, slip down over the handle and draw up round the top.

Alice's garden party parasol (Chapter 6)

You will need:

- ✂ A 13 cm (5 in) circle of lightweight cotton-type fabric (lawn is best)
- ✂ 70 cm (¾ yd) lace, 1.5 cm (⅝ in) deep
- ✂ 9 cm (3½ in) satin ribbon, 7 mm (¼ in) wide
- ✂ Matching threads
- ✂ Vilene Bondaweb
- ✂ A thin bamboo skewer, 16–18 cm (6½–7 in) long
- ✂ A coloured bead, 1 cm (⅜ in) in diameter
- ✂ Clear adhesive

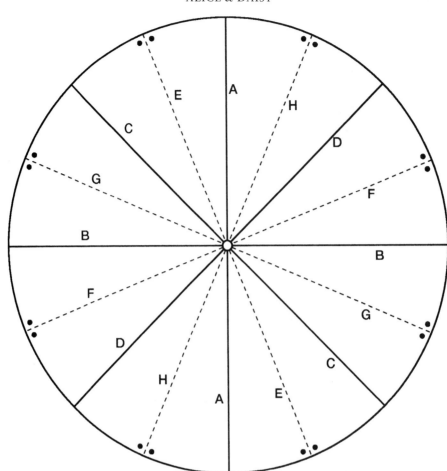

1 Trace the pattern onto Bondaweb, iron it onto the wrong side of the fabric, then cut round the edge.

2 With the right side outside (paper inside), fold the fabric in half along the solid line A: crease hard. Open out (protecting the crease) and repeat along lines B, C and D. Turn the fabric over and wrong side outside, fold and crease along the broken lines E, F, G and H in the same way.

3 Mark the centre, then discard the paper. On the wrong side and using double thread, pinch together the end of one broken line crease (the ones folding up towards you) and pass your needle through the two dots. Continue all round the circle and then go through the first one again.

4 Partially draw up, then push the skewer point down through the centre to protrude 2.5 cm (1 in), pull the thread up tightly and secure.

5   Re-crease the outer folds, then wrap them smoothly round the skewer, binding the thickest point tightly with thread to hold.

6   Join the ends of a 25 cm (10 in) length of lace, gather the straight edge, slip it over the top of the skewer and draw it up round the fabric at the thickest point. Repeat with 20 cm (8 in) lace and then 15 cm (6 in) drawn up over the cut edges. Fold 10 cm (4 in) lace in half lengthways and gather close to the folded edge. Join the cut ends and draw up tightly round the bottom.

7   Fix the bead on the top end of the skewer. Fix a butterfly bow (Trims: Chapter 9) halfway down the handle.

Daisy's picnic parasol (Chapter 6)

Follow the above directions, making the butterfly bow from 12 cm (5 in) ribbon to the same measurements as the bows of her sleeves (Step 8).

Alice's shopping umbrella (Chapter 5)

Follow the directions for Alice's parasol, but omit Steps 5 and 6: simply re-crease the outer folds neatly, and spread them evenly round the skewer as illustrated. For the bow, have points B and C each 3 cm (1¼ in) from A.

Alice and Daisy's hats

All the sisters' hats are basically boaters – a shape loved by the Edwardians. You can make a real straw boater by oversewing strands of raffia together, but this is rather laborious and the shaping can be tricky. Alice and Daisy used cereal cartons instead.

Note: Follow the appropriate diagrams to make the hat of your choice:

Hat A is worn by Daisy in Chapter 3 (Gigi)

Hat B is worn by Alice in Chapter 1 (Seaside)

Hat C is worn by Alice in Chapter 6 (Garden Party)

Hat D is worn by Daisy in Chapter 6 (Picnic)

Hat E is worn by Alice in Chapter 5 (Shopping)

You will need:

- ✂ 16 cm × 60 cm (6½ × 24 in) linen-type fabric for Hats A or D
- ✂ OR 18 cm × 65 cm (7 in × 26 in) linen-type fabric for Hat B
- ✂ OR 20 cm × 70 cm (8 in × 28 in) linen-type fabric for Hat C
- ✂ OR 15 cm × 35 cm (6 in × 14 in) felt for Hat E
- ✂ Medium-weight flexible card (cereal cartons are ideal)
- ✂ Narrow round elastic or a long elastic band
- ✂ Matching sewing threads, dry stick adhesive and clear adhesive
- ✂ *UHU Action* + fabric glue to neaten edges (optional)

1 Cut the appropriate side strip, brim and crown twice each in card, as Figs 1, 2 and 3. Glue the two brims and crowns together to make them double thickness (not the side strips).

2 Roll up a side strip, place it inside the brim and let it open out to fill the hole: mark the overlap, remove and glue the join.

3 Dry glue one side of the brim smoothly to fabric: cut level with the card round

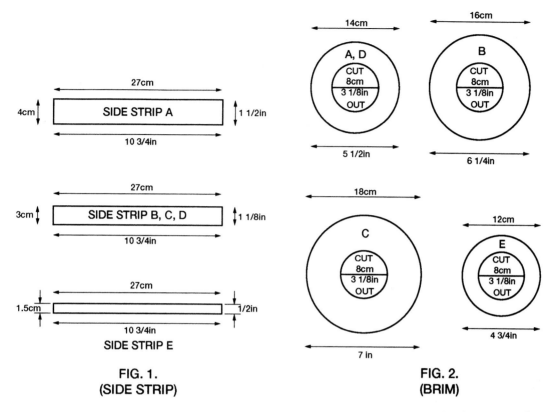

FIG. 1.
(SIDE STRIP)

FIG. 2.
(BRIM)

both edges (this is the *top*). Cover the underside also, but trim only the outer edge level. Cut a 4 cm (1½ in) diameter circle in the centre and snip the surplus fabric into tabs (Fig 4). Glue one side of the crown to the fabric and cut to leave a 1.5 cm (½ in) surplus all round, then snip out V-shaped notches to form tabs (Fig 5).

4 Place the brim underside down and smear clear adhesive on the tabs. Place the sides circle over the tabs and press them firmly up inside. Place the crown covered-side down and glue each tab. Turn and place over the sides, pressing the tabs down smoothly.

FIG. 4.

FIG. 5.

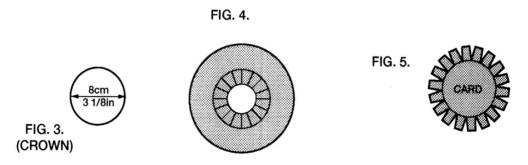

FIG. 3.
(CROWN)

5   Glue the second side strip to the fabric. Cut it level leaving a 1 cm (½ in) overlap at one end. Glue round the hat.

6   Fix elastic across under the crown, stitching it to the inner edge at each side of the brim.

Daisy's Gigi hat (Chapter 3)

Using double-sided tape, band Hat A with a 1 cm (⅜ in) wide strip of skirt fabric 5 mm (¼ in) above the brim. Add bands of 9 mm (⅜ in) wide feather-edge ribbon overlapping the edges. Finish with a double bow at the back.

Alice's seaside boater (Chapter 1)

Band hat B with 90 cm (1 yd) of 15 mm (⅝ in) wide ribbon. Make a butterfly bow (see Trims: Chapter 9) at the centre of the remaining ribbon and fix at the back.

Alice's garden party hat (Chapter 6)

Edge the brim of hat C with lace pulled quite taut. The roses (see Trims: Chapter 9) are in three shades, each a 60 cm (24 in) length of 23 mm (1 in) wide satin ribbon, set in a rosette made from 40 cm (16 in) of 50 mm (2 in) wide sheer ribbon.

Daisy's picnic hat (Chapter 6)

Bind the brim and crown of hat D with lace, as above. Band with 30 cm (12 in) of 15 mm (⅝ in) wide satin ribbon. Cut four 8 cm (3 in) lengths of 39 mm (1½ in) wide ribbon for the bow. Loop each in half (wrong side inside) and pin. Beginning at A (Fig 6) gather across to B and then from C back to A: draw up tightly round your finger. Make another bow and stitch together as Fig 7.

Gather the straight edge of 15 cm (6 in) lace and draw up round your finger. Repeat with 10 cm (4 in) lace, but draw up tightly. Stitch to the bow, with a sequin and bead in the centre. Drape 70 cm × 20 cm (28 in × 8 in) tulle or chiffon over the crown, cross under the chin and tie at the back.

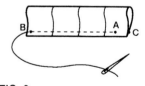

FIG. 6.

FIG. 7.

Alice's shopping hat (Chapter 5)

Glue braid round the brim of hat E and stitch lace underneath. Fix 30 cm (⅜ yd) of 9 mm (⅜ in) feather-edge ribbon round the crown. Make the front rose (see Trims: Chapter 9) from 1 m (1 yd) of 23 mm (1 in) wide satin ribbon, and the others from 2.5 m (2¾ yd) of 15 mm (⅝ in) ribbon cut into six. Stitch the large rose to the front edge of the crown, tilting down over the brim, with a horseshoe-shaped frill of sheer ribbon round the upper half.

Boutique clothes' hangers

Step-by-step diagrams show how easy the girls' pretty hangers are to make.

You will need:

- ✄ 20 cm (8 in) Flexi-wire
- ✄ 30 cm (12 in) single-face satin ribbon
- ✄ 25 cm (10 in) lace, 15 mm (⅝ in) deep
- ✄ Matching sewing threads
- ✄ Embroidered flowers, lace motifs, narrow ribbon etc. to trim
- ✄ 4 cm × 11 cm (1½ in × 4½ in) thin card
- ✄ Adhesive tape, double-sided tape (optional)
- ✄ Clear adhesive

1 Bend the wire in half (Fig 1). Clip the corners at one end of 15 cm (6 in) ribbon and fold under, then fold in half lengthways and oversew the end. Gather close to edges of ribbon (Fig 2). Push bent wire up inside ribbon and catch ends together. Draw up gathers to cover 5 cm (2 in) and secure (Fig 3).

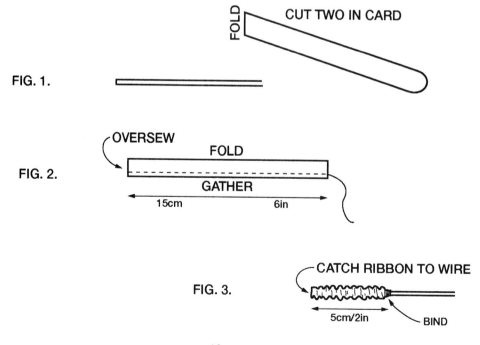

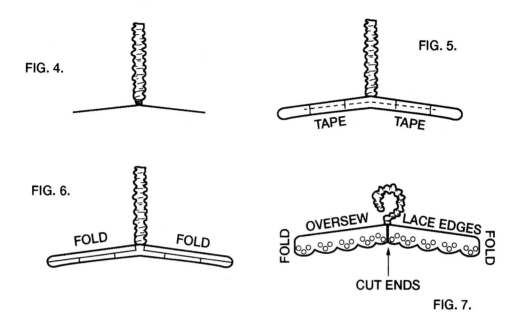

FIG. 4.

FIG. 5.

TAPE   TAPE

FIG. 6.

FOLD   FOLD

OVERSEW   LACE EDGES

FOLD   FOLD

CUT ENDS

FIG. 7.

2 Open wire out (Fig 4). Cut the pattern twice in card. Place one piece in front and one behind: tape together (Fig 5). Using double-sided tape, cover each arm with ribbon, folded lengthways over the top (Fig 6).

3 Wrap lace round to cover both sides, joining at centre front, then oversew top edges and catch together underneath (Fig 7). Bend wire into a hook (Fig 7) and trim with a tiny bow, lace, flowers etc.

Chapter 9

Pretty trims for the finishing touch

It's so simple to make beautiful satin roses, dainty butterfly bows, and even narrow braid – all from ribbon. Your miniature trimmings will always be in a perfect shade to complement the outfit and you'll save money too!

Ribbon roses

Use single-face satin ribbon, except with 3 mm (⅛ in) width, which is only double face. The 3 mm makes a charming miniature rose, but practise the technique first with wider ribbon. The *Offray* range of ribbons offers a wonderful choice of shades that are straight from nature. Alternatively, 'unnatural' colours can often look just as attractive. Dark brown or sable roses can look extremely elegant – so can navy, powder blue or grey.

1 Cut off the required length of ribbon – these amounts are a rough guide:

   Width 3 mm (⅛ in): 11 cm (4½ in)
   Width 6 mm (¼ in): 15 cm (6 in)
   Width 9 mm (⅜ in): 20 cm (8 in)
   Width 15 mm (⅝ in): 30–40 cm (12–16 in)

2 Fold the corner over, bringing A down to meet B.

3 Bring C over to meet point AB.

4 Roll the ribbon round three or four times, forming a tight tube, and stitch the bottom to hold.

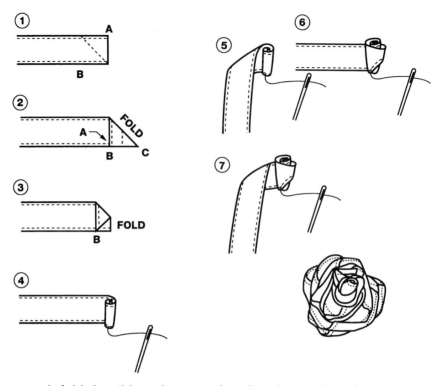

5 To make a petal, fold the ribbon down so that the edge is aligned with the tube. Then curve the ribbon around the tube to form a cone, keeping the top of the tube level with the diagonal fold.

6 When the tube again lies parallel with the remaining ribbon, take two stitches through the base to hold the petal in place.

7 Continue to make petals, sewing each one to the base of the flower before starting the next.

8 Shape the rose by gradually making the petals a little more open. Finish by tucking the end neatly underneath.

Butterfly bows

Use single- or double-face satin ribbon. The length required will depend on the ribbon width, the effect you wish to create, and whether or not you want streamers.

1 On the wrong (dull) side of the ribbon, mark point A at the centre, close to the lower edge. Mark points B and C equally either side of the centre, close to the top edge. Cut the ends in a V-shape.

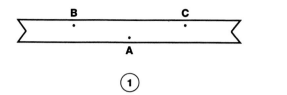

①   ②   ③

2 With the wrong side facing you, and using matching thread, bring the needle forward through point A. Then curve the left end of the ribbon round and bring the needle forward through B: curve the right end round and bring the needle forward through C. Draw up so that B and C are on top of A.

3 Take the needle up and through the centre top (point D), then take it down at the back and bring it through to the front again at point E.

4 Take the thread up over the top and wrap it tightly round the middle several times, drawing up and shaping the bow as you do so. Finish off at the back.

Plaited braid

Use 1.5 mm (1/16 in) wide satin ribbon. To estimate the amount you will need, measure the length of braid you require, then multiply it by four. For instance, to make a 15 cm (6 in) length of braid, you would require: 15 cm (6 in) × 4 = 60 cm (24 in)

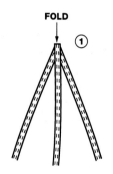

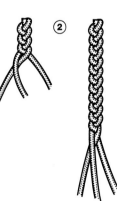

1 Fold the ribbon into three and cut one fold. Glue one end of the shorter piece inside the fold of the longer piece and pinch together.

2 Push a pin through the glued end and fix securely to something rigid. Plait very evenly, always keeping the ribbons taut and quite flat – never fold them over. Draw the plait firmly between your fingertips every 2–3 cm (inch or so) to make it smooth and even. Hold the ends with a paperclip.

3 Glue the braid into place, spreading the glue just beyond the point where you intend to cut the braid, to prevent it unravelling. Press the cut ends down well, adding a touch more glue if necessary.

Chapter 10

Bertie

Alice and Daisy are devoted to Bertie. If your dolls want a mischievous little dog too, you can grant their wish with nothing more than three woolly pompons and a few bits of felt and trimming. Almost any kind of yarn will do, but 4-ply or double-knit is easiest. Bertie's had a little mohair in it, which made his fur even fluffier!

You will need:

- ✄ 25 g (1 oz) light brown knitting yarn and a small amount of white
- ✄ 5.5 cm × 14 cm (2¼ in × 5½ in) brown felt for his ears
- ✄ Scrap of black felt for his features
- ✄ 5 cm × 10 cm (2 in × 4 in) felt and/or fabric for his jacket
- ✄ 30 cm (12 in) strong thread or fine string to tie pompons
- ✄ 10–15 cm (4–6 in) ribbon, 6–7 mm (¼ in) wide, for his bow
- ✄ 10 cm (4 in) ribbon, 6–9 mm (¼–⅜ in) wide, to fix his jacket
- ✄ 1.5 m (1½ yd) ribbon, 1.5 mm (¹⁄₁₆ in) wide, for a plaited jacket trim and collar, plus a lead OR 25 cm (10 in) narrow braid or alternative, to trim the jacket
- ✄ Plus 15 cm (6 in) ribbon, 3–7 mm (⅛–¼ in) wide, for his collar
- ✄ Plus 30 cm (12 in) ribbon, 1.5–3 mm (¹⁄₁₆–⅛ in) wide, for his lead
- ✄ Thin card, clear adhesive, large tapestry needle and small, sharp pointed scissors

  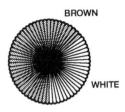

BROWN

WHITE

FIG. 1.   FIG. 2.   FIG. 3.

To make a pompon

Cut two circles of card as the pattern. Fold a 4 m (4 yd) length of yarn into four (less if the yarn is very thick) and thread the needle. Put the two circles together and wrap the yarn evenly all round the card as Fig 1. Continue going round and round, refilling the needle, until the centre is completely full as Fig 2.

Push pointed scissors through the yarn and between the card (arrow on Fig 2): cut through the yarn all round, then slip thread or string between the two cards, surrounding the yarn in the centre. Pull very tight and knot securely. Tear away the card, then trim the pompon to a neat round ball.

1   Make two pompons for the body (pattern A), using all brown yarn for the back pompon but for the front, cover two-thirds of the circle brown, and the rest white (Fig 3). Make the head pompon (pattern B) half brown and half white.

2   To join the body, divide and press back the yarn on both pompons where they

will meet (white area is the chest). Glue them firmly together (plenty of glue at the centre, easing out to nothing near the cut ends). Glue on the head as illustrated, and trim the base flat so that he stands steadily.

3   For his tail, tie eight 10 cm (4 in) lengths of yarn at the centre (with yarn), then fold in half and repeat. Fold in half again and bind the ends tightly. Poke a deep hole in the back pompon and glue the tied end into it.

4   Cut each ear twice in felt, then oversew together all round. Glue to the head.

5   Cut the eyes and nose in black felt and glue on as illustrated (trim a little yarn away underneath).

6   Cut the jacket in felt or fabric (it's a good idea to bond fabric to felt or Vilene). Make ribbon braid (Trims: Chapter 9 – reserve 30 cm [12 in] for a lead) or glue alternative trimming round the edge. Hold in place with ribbon under his tummy.

7   Make a butterfly bow (Trims: Chapter 9) for his top-knot. Glue the ends of a braid or ribbon collar round his neck. Loop one end of the lead ribbon through his collar, and glue a loop at the other to fit the doll's hand.

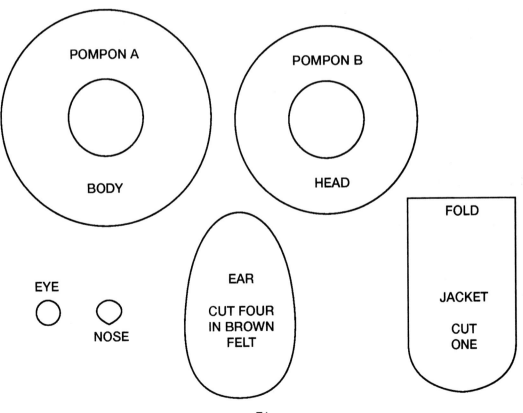

Chapter 11

Making the furniture

Alice and Daisy's furniture is basically made from cardboard and waste paper. The cheapest quality artists' mounting board is the best kind of stiff card, but you can often substitute corrugated card salvaged from delivery cartons, while cereal packets provide ideal medium-weight card. Cut it with a craft knife and a metal ruler on a cutting board. You'll need a pair of compasses too.

Making a cylindrical base

A stiff paper cylinder made from junk mail or old magazines often makes a useful foundation. Cut a hole in a piece of waste card the same diameter as your proposed cylinder. Cut long strips of medium-weight waste paper (approximately A4) the proposed height of the cylinder. Roll one up and place it inside the hole, allowing it to open up against the edge. Mark the overlap, then remove the paper and tape the join. Roll up another strip and place it inside this tube, letting it open out to fit snugly against the first sheet. Add more sheets (and then some more!) to form a rigid shell – the firmer and heavier it is, the better.

Covering fabrics

Medium-weight cotton-type fabrics are easiest to work, and a fine needlecord or velvet makes very effective upholstery.

Trimmings

Braids can be similar, or a little heavier, than those for the dolls' garments. Use a clear all-purpose adhesive.

Round tables

The table described below is 14 cm (5½ in) in diameter, but simply adjust the measurements to make it smaller or larger, or a different shape (if you are planning an oval or very big table, tape two or three cylinders together to support the top).

For the table illustrated you will need:

- ✂ A cylinder 15 cm (6 in) high × 8 cm (3 in) diameter
- ✂ Corrugated board
- ✂ Medium-weight card (cereal boxes are ideal)

74

✄ Fabric or paper to cover the top (fabric is better)

✄ 18 cm (7½ in) × 90 cm (36 in) medium-weight cotton-type fabric for the skirt

✄ 20 cm (8 in) square of medium-weight fabric, for the cloth

✄ 90 cm (1 yd) lightweight fringe 7 cm (2¾ in) deep

✄ 50 cm (20 in) ribbon, 9 mm (⅜ in) wide, to edge table-top

✄ Matching sewing threads and clear adhesive

1 Join the short edges of the skirt, then mark the top edge into eight and make two rows of gathers, 3–4 mm (⅛ in) apart.

2 Cut two 14 cm (5½ in) diameter circles of card: glue each to corrugated board and cut the board level. Rule lines across one to divide it into eight, then pin the skirt round the edge, matching the marked points. Draw up to fit and glue the surplus fabric above the gathers down over the card.

3 Cover the other circle with a larger circle of fabric or paper, turning the surplus neatly underneath. Glue on top of the first circle. Glue ribbon over the join.

4 Glue the cylinder firmly underneath, then turn up and herringbone-stitch the hem.

5 Stitch fringe round the edge of the tablecloth and drape over the table.

Upholstered chairs and footstools

Alice chose a rich garnet-coloured corduroy, while Daisy wanted a summery floral cotton – and they rang the changes with trimmings too.

Draw the patterns over 1 cm squares (the imperial measurements will be applicable). If you haven't any metric paper, rule ⅜ in squares on graph paper. Once again you can improvise with cereal and grocery cartons.

You will need:

✄ Artists' mounting board or similar weight stiff card or corrugated board

✄ Medium-weight flexible card (cereal packets are ideal)

✄ 35 cm × 60 cm (14 in × 24 in) medium-weight fabric (see above)

✄ 20 cm × 30 cm (8 in × 12 in) medium-thickness volume fleece (wadding)

✄ 1 m (1¼ yd) lightweight soft furnishing braid, 10 mm (⅜ in) wide, for the plain

chair OR 90 cm (1 yd) lightweight soft furnishing braid, 10 mm wide, and 40 cm
(½ yd) fringe, for the floral chair

✂ Matching sewing thread and clear adhesive

✂ 1 cm (⅜ in) squared paper (see above)

1 Make patterns for the back, seat and base as Fig 1 (begin with the circle, centre A),
Fig 2 and Fig 3. Cut the back and seat from medium-weight card, and the base in
board. Score the broken lines.

2 Bend the base round and glue the tabs behind the back, lower edges level (Fig 1).
Bend down the back of the seat and glue to the back (1 cm [⅜ in] below C–C), and
the base.

3 Cut a strip of medium-weight card 32 cm (12½ in) long by 9 cm (3½ in) deep, and
curve it round the base, taping the ends to the back corners. Join the seat to the
strip with bits of tape.

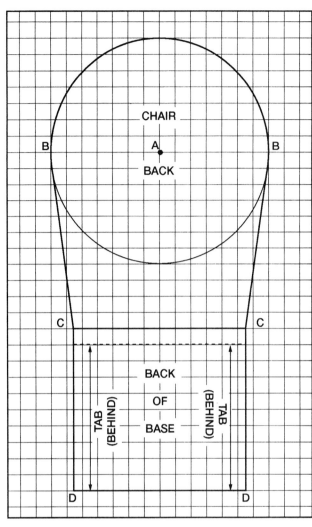

CHAIR

A

BACK

B   B

C   C

BACK

OF

BASE

TAB (BEHIND)   TAB (BEHIND)

D   D

EACH SQUARE = 1cm (3/8in)

FIG. 1.

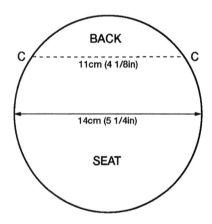

BACK

C - - - - - - - - - - - C

11cm (4 1/8in)

14cm (5 1/4in)

SEAT

FIG. 2.

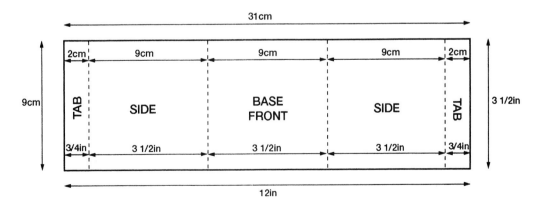

31cm

2cm   9cm   9cm   9cm   2cm

9cm

TAB   SIDE   BASE FRONT   SIDE   TAB

3 1/2in

3/4in   3 1/2in   3 1/2in   3 1/2in   3/4in

12in

FIG. 3.

4   Cut the skirt 12 cm (4½ in) deep × 40 cm (15 in) wide. Gather the top edge. Glue the side edges behind the back over the tabs, then draw up the gathers round the seat and glue to the edge, lower edge level with the base.

5   Cut the back in board. Place on the wrong side of your fabric and cut it 1.5 cm (½ in) larger all round except the lower edge D–D: cut this level. Snip the surplus round the curves into tabs, then bring it all smoothly up and glue down over the card. Glue behind the back of the chair.

6   Cut the back again in board, omitting the section below C–C. Cut the seat also, omitting the section above C–C. Cut fleece (wadding) to fit the seat and glue on top. Place the seat, fleece down, on the wrong side of the fabric and cut it 2 cm (¾ in) larger all round. Fold the surplus over the straight edge and glue. Gather the curved edge: draw up and sew or stick each corner.

7   Upholster the back section in the same way, then glue into place, followed by the seat. Glue braid and fringe into place as illustrated.

Large and small footstools

You will need:

- ✂ Thin card
- ✂ Medium-weight card
- ✂ Medium-weight scrap paper
- ✂ 15 cm × 25 cm (6 in × 10 in) medium-weight fabric for the larger stool OR 10 cm × 20 cm (4 in × 8 in) medium-weight fabric for the smaller stool
- ✂ Small pieces of thick volume fleece (wadding)
- ✂ 1 m (1⅛ yd) satin ribbon, 1.5 mm (1/16 in) wide, for the larger stool OR 75 cm (¾ yd) satin ribbon, 1.5 mm (1/16 in) wide, for the smaller stool
- ✂ Sewing thread and clear adhesive
- ✂ 4 wooden beads, 1 cm (⅜ in) diameter for feet (optional) – smaller stool only

1   Make a cylinder (see page 73) 6 cm (2½ in) diameter × 3 cm (1¼ in) high for the larger stool OR 5 cm (2 in) diameter × 1.5 cm (⅝ in) high, for the smaller one.

2   Cover the outside of the larger cylinder (not the small one) with fleece, cutting it level with the edges.

3   Cut a strip of fabric 6 cm (2½ in) × 23 cm (9 in) for the large stool OR 4 cm

(1½ in) × 18 cm (7 in) for the small one. Wrap round the cylinder, overlapping both edges, and glue the join. Snip the surplus into tabs and glue them to the paper.

4   Cut two 6 cm (2½ in) diameter circles of card for the large stool OR two 5 cm (2 in) diameter for the smaller.

5   Cut an 8 cm (3 in) diameter circle of fabric for the large stool OR 7 cm (2½ in) diameter for the smaller. Gather round the edge, then place a card circle in the centre and draw up the gathers. Repeat this step, but cut a 10 cm (4 in) circle of fabric for the large stool, or 9 cm (3½ in) for the smaller and cover the card with fleece, cutting it 1 cm (⅜ in) larger all round.

6   Glue the circles to the top and bottom of the footstool. Trim with plaited braid (Trims: Chapter 9), and glue feet under the small one.

Folding screen

Cover it with fabric, wallpaper, giftwrap or true-to-period, with lots of tiny cut-out scraps. Try to find a braid which you can cut down the centre (see Chapter 5). If not, use two widths of narrow braid side-by-side when the full width is required.

You will need:

✁   Artists' mounting board or similar weight stiff card or corrugated board
✁   Thin card and tracing paper to make a template
✁   Plain or patterned paper or fabric to cover (see above)
✁   1.7 m (1⅞ yd) braid, approx 10–12 mm (⅜–½ in) wide which can be cut in half (see above) OR 3.2 m (3⅝ yd) narrow braid, approx 5–6 mm (¼ in) wide
✁   Dry glue stick or alternative paper adhesive
✁   Clear tape, at least 12 mm (½ in) wide (a matt tape is best)
✁   Clear adhesive

1   Cut three 30 cm × 11 cm (12 in × 4½ in) pieces of board. Make a template to shape the top of each panel: mark and cut as the broken line on Fig 1.

2   Cover each panel smoothly with paper or fabric.

3   Place two panels exactly together, covered sides facing, then stick tape round one side edge to form a hinge. Open out, place covered side down and stick another length of tape over each edge of the first one. Fix the third panel in the same way.

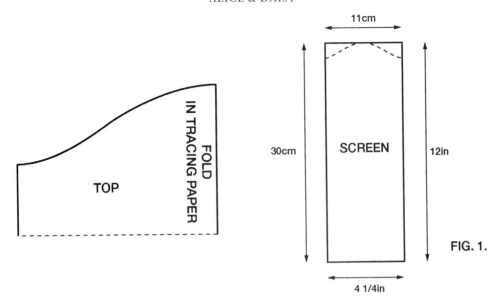

FIG. 1.

4 Glue braid round each panel as illustrated, using the full width of a wide braid (or two widths of narrow braid) round the outer side and top edges, and half-width (one width of narrow) along the inner edges.

Draped dressing table

Alice and Daisy wanted a dreamy dressing table. Kidney-shaped, flounced, draped, trimmed with lace and festooned with roses . . . surely this one is dreamy enough!

You will need:

- ✂ A sheet of artists' mounting board or similar stiff card
- ✂ Corrugated board
- ✂ Coloured paper to cover the table-top
- ✂ 16.5 cm (6½ in) medium-weight cotton-type fabric, 90 cm (36 in) wide, for the skirt
- ✂ 50 cm (½ yd) sheer voile curtain net, 90 cm (36 in) wide: 15 cm × 60 cm (6 in × 25 in) for the flounce, and 35 cm × 80 cm (12 in × 32 in) for the drapes
- ✂ 1.6 m (1¾ yd) narrow lace to trim the drapes
- ✂ 90 cm (1 yd) single-face satin ribbon, 15 mm (⅝ in) wide, for bows

80

- ✂ 1.2 m (1¼ yd) single-face satin ribbon, 9 mm (⅜ in) wide, for large roses
- ✂ 30 cm (⅜ yd) single-face satin ribbon, 7 mm (¼ in) wide, for small roses
- ✂ 3.4 m (3⅝ yd) satin ribbon, 1.5 mm (¹⁄₁₆ in) wide, to make braid OR 80 cm (1 yd) narrow braid
- ✂ White cotton tape, 10 mm wide: about 2 m (2 yd)
- ✂ Matching sewing threads
- ✂ 30–35 cm (⅜ yd) pearl trim
- ✂ A 14.5 × 10.4 cm (6 × 4 in) two-fold oval greetings card mount for the mirror
- ✂ Kitchen foil for mirror
- ✂ 40 cm (16 in) wooden dowelling, 5 mm (¼ in) in diameter
- ✂ Adhesive tape, dry stick adhesive and clear adhesive
- ✂ Victorian paper edgers to cut the mirror (optional)

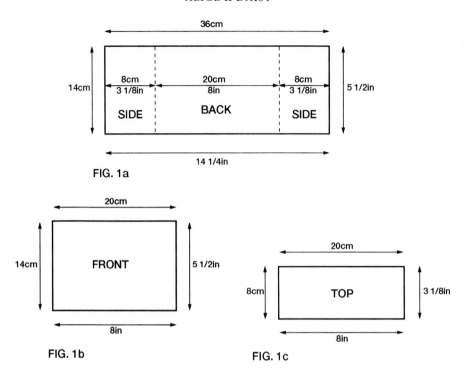

FIG. 1a

FIG. 1b

FIG. 1c

1   Cut the base in mounting board as Figs 1a, 1b and 1c.

2   Score broken lines and bend the sides forward. Tape the front in position and then the top.

3   Cut the shaped top in board and cover one side smoothly with paper. Cut the shape twice more in corrugated board and glue underneath the first piece.

4   Make a double row of gathers (divide in half) 3 mm (⅛ in) apart along the top edge of the skirt. Cut 65 cm (26 in) cotton tape: mark the centre, then mark 23 cm (9 in) each side of the centre. Mark each section into eight, mark the top edge of the skirt into sixteen. Matching the marked points, pin the lower edge of the tape over the right side of the fabric, level with the bottom row of gathers (Fig 2). Draw up the gathers and stitch.

5   Gather one long edge of the flounce, then join it to the other edge of the tape as before, but pin the tape over the wrong side of the voile (Fig 3).

6   Draw a vertical thread at the centre of the flounce, and again 12.5 cm (5 in) each side of the centre. Gather the edge, then fold the flounce in half lengthways, wrong side inside, and pin the second gathered edge level with the tape: draw up the gathers and stitch.

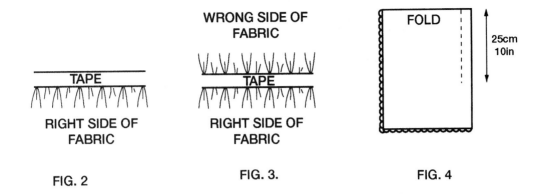

FIG. 2   **FIG. 3.**   **FIG. 4**

Gather the double voile along each drawn thread, to 1 cm (⅜ in) from the top: draw up tightly and catch over the tape. Catch the side gathers to the skirt.

7   Glue the skirt round the front and side edges of the shaped top, centres matching and top edges level. Place it on the base to mark the length of the skirt, then herringbone-stitch the hem.

8   Glue the dowelling vertically to the centre of the base back. Glue several 14 cm × 1.5 cm (5½ in × ½ in) strips of board against the dowelling to hold it firmly, then tape over it for extra security. Bind the protruding dowelling with cotton tape.

9   Glue the shaped top over the base, and the remaining tape across the back.

10   Glue plaited braid (Trims: Chapter 9) round the front and side edges.

11   Make three bows from 20 cm (8 in) lengths of ribbon (Trims: Chapter 9 – A and B each 4 cm [1½ in] from the centre) and fix over the front gathers, with a large rose (Trims: Chapter 9) made from 20 cm (8 in) ribbon in the centre of each.

12   Cut the edges of the drapes' voile along the thread to prevent fraying. Stitch lace along one long edge and both shorter ones. With the wrong side inside, fold the fabric in half and join the back edges for 25 cm (10 in) from the fold. Turn right side inside and stitch again 1.5 cm (⅝ in) from the previous line, forming a channel at the back (Fig 4). Turn right side outside.

13   Fold the front edge back 4 cm (1½ in) at the centre, then gather the centre from front to back. Draw up and wrap the thread tightly round the gathers, then catch the lace to the back point of the channel. Fix another bow and rose at the front, then slip down over the dowelling, folding back each corner 6 cm (2 in) and catching to the side.

14 Glue foil behind the window of the card mount for the mirror. Glue narrow braid and pearls round the oval, then cut a decorative edge about 1 cm (⅜ in) beyond the braid. Glue a large and two smaller roses at the top. Tape a tiny ribbon loop at the back and catch it to the drapes to hold the mirror loosely against the dowelling, with the base resting on the table at an angle.

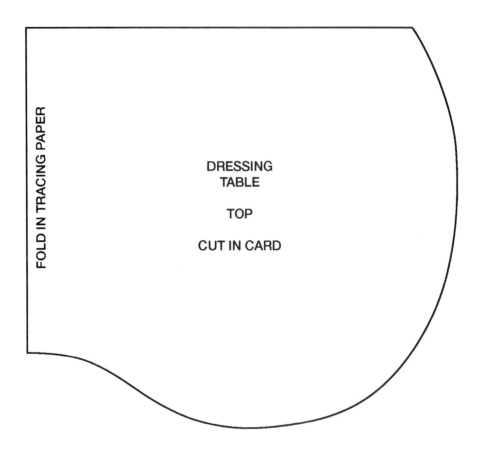

Dressing table stool

You will need:

- ✂ Paper cylinder 7–8 cm (2½–3 in) in diameter × 8 cm (3 in) high (see page 73)
- ✂ 10 cm × 20 cm (4 in × 8 in) medium-weight fabric for the skirt
- ✂ Circle of medium-weight fabric about 15 cm (6 in) diameter for seat
- ✂ 1 m (1–1⅛ yd) satin ribbon, 1.5 mm wide, to make braid OR 25 cm (¼ yd) narrow braid

- ✄ Small piece of medium-weight volume fleece (wadding)
- ✄ Matching threads and clear adhesive

Combine the directions for the table with the padded top of the footstool and glue braid above the skirt.

Stockists and suppliers

Dress fabrics (including lawn and poplin in a very good range of colours), felt, lace and embroidered edgings and trimmings, braids, beads, knitting yarns, *UHU Clear All-Purpose* and *Action* + adhesives, squared pattern-making paper and all general sewing equipment, are obtainable from branches of the John Lewis Partnership. For further information or mail order: John Lewis plc, Oxford Street, London W1A 1EX Tel: 0171 629 7711.

Offray Ribbons: for your nearest stockist, write to C.M. Offray & Son Ltd, Fir Tree Place, Church Road, Ashford, Middlesex TW15 2PH Tel: 01784 247281 or for mail order, Ribbon Designs, PO Box 382, Edgware, Middlesex HA8 7XQ Tel: 0181 958 4966.

UHU All-Purpose Clear adhesive, *UHU Stic* dry glue stick, and *UHU Action* + fabric glue are available from all good stationers and craft shops

Victorian paper edgers, and oval greetings card mounts are available from The Cutting Edge, Unit 14, CEC, Mill Lane, Coppull, Lancs. PR7 5BW Tel: 01257 792025.

Flexi-wire is obtainable from craft shops and Hewitt and Booth Ltd. Tel: 01484 546621.

Alice & Daisy

Edwardian rag doll sisters to make and dress

Valerie Janitch

(ISBN 1 85486 183 2)

This first book introduces the reader to Alice and Daisy and gives the pattern and full instructions for making the doll with a choice of hairstyles – so simple even if you have never made a rag doll before!

Charming full colour photographs follow Alice and Daisy through their busy day and whether it's lessons, shopping, tea in the country, a birthday party or just going to bed, an appropriate outfit is necessary (plus be-ribboned underpinnings, of course!). Included in the book are instructions for making a basic wardrobe consisting of camisoles, petticoats and pantalettes; nightdresses and negligées; day dresses; blouses and skirts; cloaks and bonnets together with accessories and shoes.

This title should be available from good bookshops. In the event of difficulty please contact the Books Division, Nexus Special Interests Ltd., Nexus House, Azalea Drive, Swanley, Kent BR8 8HU Tel: 01322 660070.